RED ROVER, RED ROVER!

Leabharlann na Cabraí
Cabra Library
Tel: 8691414

Kunak McGann grew up in Drogheda back in the days when electronic tablets were unheard of (she can still remember the excitement when the family got a ZX Spectrum – 'Luna Crabs', anyone?) and playing out on the street was the most fun kids could imagine. Eventually, like everyone, she had to grow up and get a proper job. So now she works in publishing and lives in Kildare with her husband, two lively sons and one chilled-out dog.

RED ROVER, RED ROVER!

WARNING!
ACTUAL PHYSICAL ACTIVITY MAY BE REQUIRED

GAMES *from an* IRISH CHILDHOOD
[THAT YOU CAN TEACH YOUR KIDS]

Kunak McGann

THE O'BRIEN PRESS
DUBLIN

Leabharlanna Poibli Chathair Baile Átha Cliath
Dublin City Public Libraries

First published 2017 by The O'Brien Press Ltd.
12 Terenure Road East, Rathgar, Dublin 6, D06 HD27, Ireland.
Tel: +353 1 4923333; Fax: +353 1 4922777
E-mail: books@obrien.ie; Website: www.obrien.ie
The O'Brien Press is a member of Publishing Ireland.

ISBN: 978-1-84717-946-3

Text © Kunak McGann 2017
Diagrams except cat's cradle © Kunak McGann 2017
Typesetting, editing, layout and design © The O'Brien Press Ltd.

6 5 4 3 2 1
20 19 18 17

All rights reserved. No part of this publication may be
reproduced or utilised in any form or by any means,
electronic or mechanical, including photocopying, recording
or in any information storage and retrieval system,
without permission in writing from the publisher.

Photographs: courtesy of Shutterstock.

Printed and bound by Gutenberg Press, Malta.
The paper in this book is produced using pulp from managed forests.

FOR MY BOYS, MILO AND ESBEN

My thanks to Joe for everything, always going above and beyond.
Thanks to Mum for her unwavering encouragement for as long as I can remember, and to Oisín, Marek, Erika and Darius for being the best playmates and partners in crime growing up. They still are. Thanks to Martha, Sarah and Ailbhe for digging up those memories of childhood rhymes (Just. Like. That.).
Thanks to all the lovely folk at The O'Brien Press for their enthusiasm for this idea from the very beginning and for letting me pick their brains on all those games (especially Claire, Helen, Bex and Elena)! And great big thanks to Emma for her creative touch, to Graham for the great cover, and to Susan for her thoughtful editing and inspired suggestions.

CONTENTS

ARE YOU COMING OUT TO PLAY?

Remember those heady days when you left the house in the morning, played out on the street or in the fields all day long and didn't come back in until teatime? Sometimes it was just two of you playing Kerbs or Sevens, practising hard, or maybe a few more of you wearing holes in your socks playing Skipping or Elastics.

On rainy days, it was retreating inside for Murder in the Dark, Boy/Girl or Battleship. But then there was that perfect day, when the sun was shining, when everyone seemed to be at a loose end, when the older kids didn't mind playing with the younger ones for once, and someone suggested Bulldog or Red Rover; and you will forever remember the unadulterated joy of charging recklessly across a field with your best pals by your side, or of swooping in at the end of a game of Forty Forty or Tip the Can with an 'I save all!'

Some of the games in this book are safe as houses and some are downright dodgy, but nearly all of the time, nearly all of the kids will be just fine. These games are versions I used to play (with varying degrees of success, and varying numbers of bumps and bruises) back in the 1980s. Growing up on an estate of about forty houses, most of which had at least two kids, there was rarely a shortage of playmates. There was never a shortage of ideas for games either, the range of which I didn't quite appreciate until I started putting pen to paper.

This is not an official directory, and the versions I explain here may differ a little – or a lot – from what you played yourself. Why not use this collection as inspiration to dig up your own memories of the games you played way back when, and go outside and play them with the children in your life.

TEAM
GAMES

RED ROVER

WHAT YOU'LL NEED

A gang of kids – eight at the very least, but better with lots more – and an open area to play in.

THE BIG IDEA

Players are divided into two teams that stand facing each other, holding hands in a chain (sounds romantic, but it isn't). One team picks a player from the opposite team and shouts at the top of their voice (*Braveheart*-style): 'Red Rover, Red Rover, we call Sean over'. Sean then runs at full pelt towards their chain, attempting to break through a pair of held hands. If he manages to, he gets to choose a member of that team to come back and join his team with him. If he doesn't, he joins their team.

BEST STRATEGY

◆ Spreading your biggest/strongest players across the team makes sense.

◆ When picking someone to call over, choose the person least likely to have the strength, body mass or fast-moving momentum to break your hand-holding chain.

PHYSICAL RISK – 9/10

Most of the risk rests with the smaller/slighter players, who are targeted as the weak link in a chain (no matter what kind of giant, yeti-like pal is holding their hand). So, no problem there, then.

SURVIVAL TIPS

◆ Should generally be played on a smooth and, if at all possible, soft surface. Avoid playing on solid concrete or roads with vicious potholes, or near any sort of vertical structures (brick walls, telegraph poles, etc.).

◆ Oh, and that little girl from No. 8 that looks like she's the weak link has a grip like you wouldn't believe and will die before she lets you through.

OVERALL PLAYABILITY

This can be a rough game, but it's easy to grasp the rules, and has great playability. Generally only finishes up when all the big guys end up on the one team, or there's a definite, have-to-report-this-to-the-parents kind of injury.

RELIEVO/ CAPTURE THE FLAG

WHAT YOU'LL NEED

Enough players to make up two teams of *at least* four each (but much better with more), and a play area big enough for two jails and plenty of space in between. For Capture the Flag, you'll also need a flag (or T-shirt, etc.).

THE BIG IDEA

The name of this game has a few variations depending on where you grew up – Relevio, Relievo, Ringolevio - but for us it was always 'Lievo!' Players are split into two teams, and each team has a 'jail' or 'den' (a marked-out area in a field or between two pillars, etc.). The object of the exercise is to catch opposing team members and put them in jail, while evading capture yourself. Those of a more heroic bent can make a solo-run to the other team's jail, shout 'Relievo!' and free all their jailed team mates. The team that manages to capture all of the other team wins (and lords it over them for days).

VARIATION

A variation of this game, Capture the Flag, has the added objective of getting hold of the other team's (hidden) flag. Grab that flag and win the game.

BEST STRATEGY

◆ Sneakiness is a great asset for this game – either while tracking your prey, or trying to keep a low profile and staying out of jail – and nothing will top the execution of a co-ordinated surprise attack on the other team's jail.

◆ Catching the other team is important, but keeping them in jail is equally important, so have your most solid and formidable players as jailers, while your fastest, sneakiest runners are out catching.

PHYSICAL RISK – 5/10

A lot of this game can involve either standing around in jail, or standing around guarding people in jail, and the physical risk is mostly in the hot pursuit of someone, or when you're running for your life.

SURVIVAL TIPS

Find out what you're good at in this game and stick with it. If you're fast, get out catching; if you're buff, get to jailing. If you're neither fast nor buff, probably best to hang close to your own jail and bask in the reflected menace of your beefy jailers.

OVERALL PLAYABILITY

This is playground war and, like war, can go on much longer than it should. The more tactical the play, the more exciting it is for everyone. With two evenly-matched teams going head-to-head, Relievo can go on for hours.

CHARGE!

WHAT YOU'LL NEED

No point in playing this game without A LOT of kids. And you'll need a large area for teams to charge at each other.

THE BIG IDEA

This game is similar to Relievo, with the emphasis very much on the opening act. A few kids stomp around the estate or school playground, rallying the troops with the cry, 'Line up for Charge! Line up for Charge!' Others join them in the shouting and stomping (this is one of the most fun parts of Charge!). Once a critical mass is achieved, the assembled crowd divides up into two teams. Back in the day, the teams were boys against girls. The key is to divide quickly and not lose the momentum. Decide on a jail and then line up at either end of a field, open area or playground. After a short-lived face-off and some trash talk, the teams run full pelt at one another. Catch opposing team members and put them in your marked-out jail, or rescue your team mates from a similar fate. To be honest: after all the stomping, shouting and trash-talking, the game usually runs out of steam fairly quickly after the initial charge.

BEST STRATEGY

There are political lessons to be learned here: get some of the most popular kids on board early on or your attempts to whip up a game will fall on deaf ears.

PHYSICAL RISK – 5/10

With most of the fun of this game concentrated at the beginning, before there's any possibility of physical contact, this is a safe enough bet. The longer the game goes on, the higher the physical risk.

SURVIVAL TIPS

If the game actually gets to the charge, those leading it usually fare the worst. So unless you're pretty zippy on your feet, or one of the more rugged on the playground, hang back and try and survive the first wave of attacks.

OVERALL PLAYABILITY

Charge! tends to be a fairly short-lived game, unless it morphs into a more strategic game of Relievo. All good, rabble-rousing fun, though.

ROUNDERS

WHAT YOU'LL NEED

Players to make up two teams of at least five each, a bat (baseball/cricket bat, hurley or tennis racquet) and ball (tennis ball or sliotar), a large playing area, and cones or jackets for each of the four bases.

THE BIG IDEA

A cross between baseball and cricket, the bat-and-ball game of Rounders was most likely the forerunner of baseball. Our cash-strapped 1980s version used a wooden tennis racquet and ball, and jumpers or jackets marking out a diamond of first, second and third bases and home. Teams take turns batting and fielding. The fielders designate a pitcher to throw the ball to the batter, who has three attempts to hit it (or they're out) and then drop the 'bat' and run like a demon to first base (or further if they can manage it). Then it's the next batter's turn, and when they run to first base, the player who went before them runs on to second base, and so on. Once a batter makes it to a base, they're safe, but if they or the base they're running to is hit by the ball, or a fielder catches the ball they've hit, they're out. Our version had the whole batting team out if a fielder catches with one hand, or when the batting team has three players out.

SCORING

We scored a point for each player that makes it all the way around the bases, and two points for a 'rounder', where a batter runs all the way around the diamond in the one go.

DID YOU KNOW?

When we were growing up, I think most of us were blissfully unaware that Rounders is one of the four official sports of the GAA (along with football, hurling and handball). You can find out more about the official version on their website, www.gaarounders.ie.

BEST STRATEGY

◆ When fielding, it's important to have reliable catchers posted at each of the bases.

◆ When batting, decide on an order that makes sense. There's no point in having your fastest runner stuck behind one of your slowest (as they can't pass them out).

PHYSICAL RISK – 3/10

The only real danger comes from bullish fielders or batters, or if a player is incapable of stepping out of the trajectory of a ball falling at high velocity (which can sometimes be trickier than it sounds).

SURVIVAL TIPS

◆ Watch out for the fielders who throw the ball at you with more force than is strictly necessary.

◆ Stand well back from where an exuberant batter might throw the tennis racquet before they set off around the diamond – the shin bone can take a bad bruise that way.

OVERALL PLAYABILITY

Rounders is great fun, particularly if it's competitive but not too competitive. It can work really well with a mix of ages/abilities. Watch out for fielders getting a bit bored (long-term fielders have been known to lie down on the job).

BALL
GAMES

SCOT/SPUD

WHAT YOU'LL NEED

Four players or more, a tennis ball and a bit of space for everyone to run around in.

THE BIG IDEA

Each player has six lives, and the aim is to deplete the other players' lives by hitting them with the ball. When someone catches or picks up the ball, they shout 'Scot!' With that, all the players have to freeze and they can't move until the ball is thrown again. Whenever the ball isn't actually in someone's hands, it's up for grabs by anyone. Each time you're hit, you lose a life, and if someone manages to catch your throw with two hands, you lose two lives. If a catcher extraordinaire manages to use just one hand to catch your throw, that's it, you're out.

VARIATION

In Spud, each player is given a number. While everyone else runs away, the person who's 'on' throws the ball up and, at the height of the throw, calls out a number. The player whose number was called has to run back and retrieve the ball. Once they do, they shout, 'Spud!' and everyone must freeze. The player with the ball then tries to hit one of the other players with it, and if they do, that player gets a letter ('S' for their first hit, then 'P', then 'U', and finally 'D') and is 'on' for the next round. If they miss, the player who threw it is 'on'. Once someone gets a 'D', they're out of the game.

BEST STRATEGY

◆ Remain a respectful distance from everyone, but close enough so that you might be able to hit them with a ball if it comes your way – it's a balancing act!

◆ Stay out of the way of the 'best thrower'.

◆ Spend all your waking hours practising catching a tennis ball with one hand.

PHYSICAL RISK – 6/10

Unfortunately, the easier a target you are in this game, the more physical risk you're likely to encounter.

SURVIVAL TIPS

Unspoken and technically illegal, strategic coalitions are useful in this game. If you show a little generosity to a particular player by aiming at someone else, they might just return the favour.

OVERALL PLAYABILITY

Lots of fun to be had with this one, and games are known to include tens of players. To add a bit of spice, play as twilight approaches, when the difficulty level rises exponentially every five minutes.

KERBS/KERBY

WHAT YOU'LL NEED

Two players, one football and a quiet road (with kerbs).

THE BIG IDEA

This game is an absolute 80s classic. The central idea is very simple: two players stand on opposite sides of the road and throw a football to hit the kerb on the other side. Imaginative variations come into play with the scoring: 10 points for a simple kerb hit, 20 points if the ball then rolls back to your own kerb, 50 points if you catch the ball on the rebound, and 100 points if you score a hit by throwing the ball backwards over your head. After the initial hit, players then move to the centre of the road and use one-handed throws to hit the curb for 5 points each, only losing their turn when they finally miss one. Players should agree on what each throw scores, as well as the winning score, before the game starts.

BEST STRATEGY

While everyone admires the show-boater in kerbs (who doesn't love to see someone get the backwards throw just right?), the steady players usually take the crown in Kerbs.

PHYSICAL RISK – 2/10

Traffic is probably the biggest danger here. No.1: look for a safe place (a quiet road or cul-de-sac is probably best). Make sure everyone studies up on the Green Cross Code before you start, and you're all set.

SURVIVAL TIPS

Practise, practise, practise. The more you play this game, the better you get – even for those of us with limited sporting ability. Sure, there are other things to do in the world, but that kid who was seen playing Kerbs on his own from dawn to dusk was climbing his way up the neighbourhood rankings.

OVERALL PLAYABILITY

For such a simple game, many a long summer's day was devoted entirely to Kerbs. And while only two people can play at a time, it wasn't uncommon to see several games going on simultaneously on the same road, either separately or as part of an epic championship. Top marks for playability.

SPACE INVADERS

WHAT YOU'LL NEED

At least three players (better with more), a high wall and a tennis ball.

THE BIG IDEA

Drawing on the universally-loved computer game, one player attempts to hit the other players with a tennis ball as they take turns running across a short distance in front of a high wall. Once you're hit, you're out. Last one out is 'on' for the next game. (To make it last longer, each player can have a number of lives to lose before they're out.)

DID YOU KNOW?

Space Invaders was first released in the late 1970s and, with *Star Wars* proving such a hit the year before, brought new sci-fi elements to the popular shoot-'em-up format. It was the first shooting game to have targets fire back at players, the first where players had multiple lives, and the first to save a player's score (which soon led to years of kids using naughty combinations of three letters to fill up those high score tables – remember?).

BEST STRATEGY

Be really, really good at aiming at moving targets. And run, run like the wind.

PHYSICAL RISK – 7/10

If you're slow or not very good at dodging a ball thrown at you (often with some venom), you could be looking at a nasty bruise or two.

SURVIVAL TIPS

◆ Make sure you specify the distance that the person who's 'on' has to stand from the wall (or else it'll be a bloodbath).

◆ Try not to make any real enemies on the street – 'cos this is their chance to hit you really, really hard and not have you run and tell.

OVERALL PLAYABILITY

Dead simple. And who doesn't love Space Invaders?

DODGEBALL

WHAT YOU'LL NEED

Between eight and sixteen players, depending on the space available, and between two and six dodgeballs (the official ones are nice and soft and made of foam or rubber). You'll also need a way of marking out the rectangle (chalk or cones, etc.).

THE BIG IDEA

Mark out a rectangle with a central dividing line, with players on two equal teams remaining in their team's half for the entire game. Before play starts, the balls are placed along the central line. In the opening rush, players run to retrieve these dodgeballs, but are not allowed throw them immediately and must pass them back to a teammate.

The object of the game is then to hit members of the opposing team below the shoulders with a ball – if you hit someone directly (without the ball bouncing off the floor, wall, etc.), and no one catches it, that player is out of the game. But if that player catches your ball (and holds it for at least two seconds), you're out. If you hit a player and one of their teammates catches the ball on the rebound, you're out, your target stays in, and one of their eliminated players gets 'resurrected'.

You can use a held ball to block a hit, but if you hold onto a ball for more than ten seconds, you're out and must roll the ball over to the other team. Players can pick up dead balls in their own half and throw them back at the other team, but if you go outside the boundaries to retrieve a dead ball, you must wait to throw until you're back in your half. Once one team has all players eliminated, the game is over.

VARIATIONS

◆ When Dodgeball is played on a basketball court, a player's whole team is resurrected if they manage to score a basket or hit the opposition's basketball board.

◆ And a 'No Lines' rule can be introduced for games with only a few players left on the court, when dodging is easier, so players can move anywhere within the rectangle to get a better shot.

BEST STRATEGY

◆ Co-ordinate with the rest of your team – several balls thrown at the same time from different parts of a team's half are much harder to dodge.

◆ Aim low (between the thigh and the shin), where it's harder to catch.

PHYSICAL RISK – 8/10

Dodgeballs are designed to minimise the hurt, but this is a game where hitting the other players is the whole idea.

SURVIVAL TIPS

As counter-intuitive as it sounds, don't hide behind other team members, or you'll never see the ball coming when they dodge out of the way.

OVERALL PLAYABILITY

Fast-paced, frenetic fun, particularly for older kids and teenagers.

MARBLES

WHAT YOU'LL NEED

Players will need their own marbles (anything up to a dozen each), and a small patch of tarmac/concrete where you can draw a circle (with chalk or a stone).

THE BIG IDEA

A simple game this, but with increasingly practised and skilled players, a very enjoyable one. A circle is drawn in chalk on a level driveway or path and, to set up, each player rolls an agreed number of their marbles into random positions inside the circle. Then players take turns rolling more marbles in, doing their best to knock other marbles out of the circle. Any they manage to hit out, they keep.

There are a number of different methods for rolling your marble: you can form a fist and tuck your thumb under your index finger and flick the marble with your thumb, you can simply put the marble in your cupped palm and tip up your hand to roll the marble off, or you can put your marble on the ground and flick it with your index finger (much like you would flick an annoying little brother's ear, say).

A player's turn ends when they fail to knock any marbles out. And the game ends when there are no more marbles to be knocked out of the circle.

BEST STRATEGY

While there can be a bit of luck involved in this game, it's mostly about skill and practise. If you're lacking in skill, you've got to make up for it in practise.

PHYSICAL RISK – 3/10

Injuries in this game are mostly self-inflicted, from poorly judged marble flicks. Don't underestimate just how painful it can be to flick your finger full force against tarmac.

SURVIVAL TIPS

Most importantly, decide before anyone does anything whether the game is a friendly, or whether it's keepsies (where players get to keep whatever marbles they knock out of the circle). Many a good friendship has been ruined by lack of clarity on the rules of Marbles.

OVERALL PLAYABILITY

A simple game that can become seriously addictive.

QUEENIE I-O

WHAT YOU'LL NEED

A small ball (tennis ball or similar), and at least five children.

THE BIG IDEA

One person is 'on', as Queenie, and stands with their back to everyone else lined up about three metres or so behind them (the older the players, the further the distance). Queenie throws the ball backwards over their head towards the other players, who scramble to get it. If one of them manages to catch it before it bounces on the ground, they shout 'Caught the ball, I-O!', and they become Queenie. Otherwise, once it's been caught everyone lines up again, hands behind backs (including the person who is now hiding the ball). They chant:

Queenie I-O, who has the ball?
Are they short or are they tall?
Are they fat or are they thin?
Or are they like a rolling pin?

With that, Queenie turns around and, doing their best Sherlock Holmes, tries to work out who has the ball. If they guess correctly, they stay on. If not, the person that has the ball becomes Queenie. Another version has Queenie 'on' until one catcher manages to be the last person picked as having the ball.

BEST STRATEGY

◆ The best possible strategy is to catch the ball before it bounces, so ball skills play a role here.

◆ After that, it's all about playing it cool while you have the ball, so those who are better at bluffing – the better liars, in other words – will fare best. What better than a children's game that rewards lying?

PHYSICAL RISK – 3/10

The risk is in the initial scramble for the ball; if there is a range of children of different ages playing, the smaller ones can get trampled.

SURVIVAL TIPS

If you can stand it, step back from the tussle for the ball and hope that it rebounds from someone's hands. Statistically, it's bound to head in your direction eventually, if you play long enough.

OVERALL PLAYABILITY

This is fun while it lasts, but younger children will probably need someone to help them run the game, while it won't keep older children occupied for too long.

DONKEY

WHAT YOU'LL NEED

A ball (a football works well), and can be played with as few as three children.

THE BIG IDEA

Players stand in a circle throwing the ball to one another. If you drop the ball when it's thrown to you, you're 'D'. Another drop and you're 'D-O', another and you're 'D-O-N', all the way to 'D-O-N-K-E-Y' and you're out. For younger kids, it's probably best to throw in an orderly fashion around the circle (from one player to the next, to the next) while older players can choose to throw to random people across the circle, so there's an element of unpredictability.

For an even more punitive version of Donkey (with added hilarity), players can lose the use of limbs or eyes when they drop the ball – so players have to stand on one leg once they're 'D', also have to close one eye when 'D-O', or use only one arm, etc. The rules can be decided on by all the players before the game begins.

BEST STRATEGY

◆ Ball skills are of primary importance here. Can you throw and catch? If so, you're off to a great start.

◆ As the game gets more complicated, other required skills are tracking the ball (when it's being thrown to random players), bluffing (pretending to throw the ball to one player, then throwing to another), and the complex technical abilities involved in catching a ball thrown at you with speed, while you're standing on only one leg and using only one eye (or even with both eyes closed, in more daredevil games).

PHYSICAL RISK – 4/10

The younger version of this game is fairly safe, bar the odd stray ball hitting some poor unfortunate child in the face. The older version of the game has added danger, naturally.

SURVIVAL TIPS

It sounds obvious, but in longer games you can easily forget to be ready – stay alert! Always know where the ball is, and be ready to catch it.

OVERALL PLAYABILITY

This is a game better suited to young children, although not so young that they struggle to throw or catch, or that they can't spell D-O-N-K-E-Y. Older children will tend to get bored with it quite easily (hence the improvised rules for the more grown-up version). But there is a window of a few years where kids get great enjoyment out of this one.

PIGGY IN THE MIDDLE

WHAT YOU'LL NEED

Three children and a ball (a football is probably best but can be played with any size).

THE BIG IDEA

One child throws a ball to another, while a third (the piggy in the middle) stands in between them and tries to intercept and catch the ball. If they do, they switch place with the thrower, who becomes piggy in the middle.

Traditionally, this is a game for just three players, but it can accommodate more if you want to have more than one piggy in the middle or more than one child on each side, throwing and catching (both of these options ensure a more chaotic game, which is often the object of the exercise). Otherwise, extra children can wait their turn to be substituted in for a thrower who's caught out.

BEST STRATEGY

Strategy depends on who your catcher is, and who your piggy is. If the piggy in the middle is on the tall side, you're going to have to practise a little distraction and misdirection (like a striker trying to put off a goalie when taking a penalty).

PHYSICAL RISK – 4/10

A relatively safe game, although the risk rating increases with the number of players and corresponding level of chaos.

SURVIVAL TIPS

Pick your playmates carefully. There's nothing quite as miserable as being stuck as the piggy in the middle for ages, while two gloating players pass the ball easily over your head.

OVERALL PLAYABILITY

Better for younger children, but if their throwing and catching isn't up to snuff, they'll need an adult or older child to help them out.

A IS FOR ...

WHAT YOU'LL NEED
A ball that's easy to bounce repeatedly (a football or basketball), and two
players or more.

THE BIG IDEA
This game combines brains and some ball skills, and is suited to a small number
of players. The basic idea is to bounce the ball steadily while chanting: 'A! My
name is Angela, my husband's name is Alf, we live in Australia and we sell
Apples.' (Boys might prefer to use a boy's name first and a wife's second.)
Then on to B, C, D and so on, with each player coming up with new names,
countries and sale items for each letter, on the bounce of the ball. If they drop
the ball, or fail to come up with a word in time for the next bounce, it's the
other player's turn.

BEST STRATEGY
The more you play this game, the wider a repertoire of names, countries
and consumables you build up. And it might be an idea to mutually agree
beforehand on leaving out X.

PHYSICAL RISK – 2/10
This level of risk is purely because if you're playing on hard ground (on your
front drive or out on the road) to get a good bounce, there's a chance you
might be concentrating so much on thinking up names that you miss a bounce
and the ball hits you in the face.

SURVIVAL TIPS

Apart from dropping the ball, you have to watch out for tricky letters. It's always good to have go-to words for Q and Z.

OVERALL PLAYABILITY

This is a good game to play when you can only muster up a friend or two. And who says you have to stick with names, countries and products? Use your imagination and make things as interesting as you like.

SEVENS

WHAT YOU'LL NEED
Two players or more and a tennis ball.

THE BIG IDEA
Taking turns, each player throws the ball against a wall in the following sequence:

- Onesies (done once): throw straight to the wall and catch.
- Twosies (done twice); throw against the wall, allowing one bounce and back into the hands.
- Threesies (done three times, you get the picture): throw against the wall, but clapping once before you catch it.
- Foursies: throw to the wall, allowing one bounce and spinning around before you catch the ball.
- Fivesies: clap your hands behind your back before the catch.
- Sixies: touch the ground.
- Sevensies: jump up and clap.

You can change the different throws, depending on the skill level of the players. When you drop the ball, it's over to the next player. You must complete all seven throws in one turn to win. Once you've done that, you can add in more difficult rounds – where all seven throws are done with one hand, under a leg, with eyes closed, etc.

BEST STRATEGY

- Mr Miyagi-like concentration required here. Don't let the other players' chit-chatting behind you put you off.
- And make sure the rules you agree on are the best ones for you. If you struggle with co-ordinating different types of movement into one quick throw (eg throwing, jumping and clapping), stick with more straightforward variations.

PHYSICAL RISK – 2/10

The most risk in this game comes from being hit by spinning players or stray balls.

SURVIVAL TIPS

- Stand back a bit and give the other players room.
- Avoid playing against a pebble-dash wall; there's no telling where the ball will go.

OVERALL PLAYABILITY

Simple rules for this one, but it can get very competitive, particularly with two evenly-matched players.

JACKS

WHAT YOU'LL NEED

Two players or more, a patch of flat ground, a small rubber ball and a set of ten jacks (small six-pointed stars of metal or plastic). If you're on a budget, you can use stones instead of jacks, but it does make things considerably more difficult.

THE BIG IDEA

To decide who goes first, you 'flip' the jacks from your palm onto the back of your hand, then back again, and see who can hold onto the most jacks. You then start the game by scattering the jacks on the ground, and each player takes turns using one hand to throw the ball up, pick up the required number of jacks and catch the ball after just one bounce. For each round, the player must pick up all the jacks in this way, transferring the picked-up jacks to their other hand after each throw. So for 'Onesies', one jack ten times, for 'Twosies', five sets of two jacks, for 'Threesies', three sets of three jacks and then the leftover jack, etc. If they let the ball bounce more than once, or fail to pick up the correct number of jacks, their go is over. First to conquer 'Tensies' is the winner.

VARIATION

To make it more interesting, you can vary the rules a bit: No Bouncies, Double Bouncies, Left-handed (or Right-handed for the citeogs), or the deadly Black Widow (you have to go from Onesies all the way up to Tensies without making a single mistake, or you start from the beginning again).

DID YOU KNOW?

This game comes from the age-old Knucklebones, which used small pieces of sheep bones.

BEST STRATEGY

◆ When throwing the jacks down, aim to have them spread out a little, but not too far apart, otherwise picking up the right number of them is going to be tricky.

◆ When throwing the ball up, give it enough height so that you've got time to pick up the jacks, but not so much that you can't control where it's going to bounce.

PHYSICAL RISK – 3/10

Scuffing your hand on the ground when you reach for the jacks is as bad as it should get. (Playing with stones instead of jacks increases this risk substantially.)

SURVIVAL TIPS

When not playing, keep the jacks out of reach of babies and toddlers. You don't want one of those bad boys showing up in a GI x-ray.

OVERALL PLAYABILITY

Jacks was hugely popular in the '60s and '70s, though its appeal had waned somewhat by the 1980s. But it has the same charm as games like Sevens and Marbles – if you're bitten by the bug, you can spend hours practising.

ROPE/ STRING GAMES

ELASTICS/FRENCH ELASTICS/CHINESE SKIPPING

WHAT YOU'LL NEED

At least three players, and a length of thick elastic (or lots of smaller elastic bands strung together) tied to form a loop that's a couple of metres long.

THE BIG IDEA

Two players stand inside the loop, with the elastic fairly tight around their ankles ('holding the elastics'). Another player starts to jump between the two sides of the loop while chanting:

England
(The jumper starts outside the elastics and jumps in to land with feet either side of the left elastic.)
Ireland
(Jump to land feet either side of the right elastic.)
Scotland
(As for England.)
Wales
(As for Ireland.)

Inside
(Jump to land both feet inside the loop.)
Outside
(Jump to land both feet outside the loop.)
Donkeys'
(Jump to land both feet inside the loop again.)
Tails
(Jump onto the two strands of elastic, with your feet holding them down to the ground, one foot on each.)

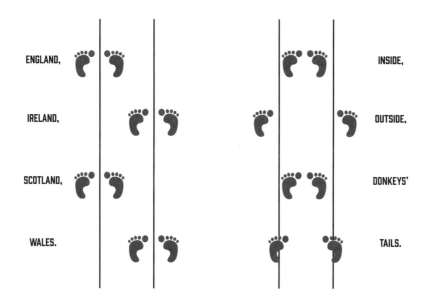

ENGLAND,			INSIDE,
IRELAND,			OUTSIDE,
SCOTLAND,			DONKEYS'
WALES.			TAILS.

Miss any of the actions, and it's your turn to hold the elastics. If you manage to get through the first round unscathed, you move up to 'Kneesies' (where the elastics are at knee-height), then up to 'Thighsies', 'Bumsies', 'Waisties' and as far up as is practical. You haven't lived until you've seen someone trying 'Under Armsies' and 'Necksies', which basically involves a lot of can-canning. (Could that be where the name French Elastics came from?)

VARIATIONS

◆ Other rhymes include: '2-4-6-8, Sitting on the cottage gate, Eating cherries off a plate, 2-4-6-8' and 'Banana split, Banana split, Banana, Banana, Banana split', with feet landing on the elastics for '8' and 'split'.

◆ We also had rounds called 'Runnies' (where players jog on the spot throughout) 'Hopsies', all done on one foot, 'Skinnies' and 'Widies', where the two sides of the elastic loop are very close together or far apart, and 'Blindies', done without the luxury of sight.

BEST STRATEGY

Repeat, repeat, repeat to perfect. If you find yourself friendless one day, why not use a couple of chairs to hold the elastics while you practise?

PHYSICAL RISK – 6/10

While it's all fairly safe at the lower levels of Elastics, players throw caution to the wind when attempting the higher-up levels. And let's not even talk about 'Blindies' – whose idea was that?

SURVIVAL TIPS

Because shoes can catch on elastics, a lot of children choose to play this one in stocking feet – have a plan to sneak those torn-up socks past the parents.

OVERALL PLAYABILITY

Outstanding. Right up there with Kerbs for popularity and playability.

COLOURS IN THE RAINBOW

WHAT YOU'LL NEED
A skipping rope and at least five players.

THE BIG IDEA
Two players are 'on' and they each pick a colour. Holding each end of a skipping rope, they move it across the ground (like a slithering snake). Other players take turns jumping over the rope, shouting a colour. If they stand on the rope, they're out. If they shout a colour chosen by one of the two players that are 'on', that player drops the rope and runs after them. If the shouter manages to get back to the rope without being caught, it's their turn to hold the rope and choose a colour.

BEST STRATEGY
◆ If you like holding the rope, choose an obscure colour. (We had rules outlawing colours like 'mint green' and 'puce'!)
◆ If you're jumping, watch those slithering ropes.

PHYSICAL RISK – 3/10
A bit of running and jumping never killed anyone. Or did it?

SURVIVAL TIPS
After the first few rounds, it's really a case of surviving the boredom that sets in.

OVERALL PLAYABILITY
There are plenty of more exciting games out there, but this can be good for younger players who are keen to show off their knowledge off colours.

SKIPPING

WHAT YOU'LL NEED
At least three players and a long length of thick rope.

THE BIG IDEA
Ah, the classic! Two people hold a long rope, one at each end, and move their arms in sync in regular circles so that the rope swings high enough to fit a person or two in the middle, jumping the rope each time it comes around. As soon as the jumper trips, they're out (and have to take their turn at holding one end of the rope).

Songs to accompany the skipping are as varied as the kids' imaginations. Here are just a few examples:

VOTE FOR DE VALERA
Vote, vote, vote for De Valera
(Skipper 1, Conor, skipping on his own.)
In comes Jamie at the door
(Skipper 2, Jamie, has to run in and skip alongside Conor.)
Jamie is the one that will have a lot of fun
And we don't need Conor any more
(Conor runs out.)

TEDDY BEAR, TEDDY BEAR
Teddy bear, teddy bear, touch the ground
Teddy bear, teddy bear, turn around
Teddy bear, teddy bear, climb the stairs
Teddy bear, teddy bear, say your prayers
(All with actions to match.)

JELLY ON A PLATE

Jelly on a plate, jelly on a plate,
Wibble wobble, wibble wobble,
Jelly on a plate.

This rhyme has lots of possible verses (sausages or pancakes in a pan, candles on a cake, sweeties in a jar) and allows for lots of hilarious actions for wibble wobble and sizzle sizzle, etc.

BEST STRATEGY

Skipping involves jumping up and down in a constant rhythm. If you're good at that, you're all set. If you suffer in any way from anti-rhythm or a lack of grace, you're doomed.

PHYSICAL RISK – 5/10

The worst that can happen to you in this game is tripping over the rope and falling to the ground. Your level of physical risk is inversely proportional to your skill at breaking your own fall and how much practice you've had at it.

SURVIVAL TIPS

A single skipping rope won't be long enough; you'll need something longer. But don't be tempted to tie two wooden-handled skipping ropes together – this ensures that the centre of the new rope has a large, wooden weapon moving at speed towards the skipper's head for each revolution. Bound to end in tears.

OVERALL PLAYABILITY

An afternoon to master, a lifetime to enjoy. Kids can play this for HOURS. Everyone has to wait their turn, and by changing songs (each one requiring slightly different actions), there's plenty of variety.

HEIGHTS

WHAT YOU'LL NEED

A length of rope and at least three players (better with more).

THE BIG IDEA

A simple premise: two players hold a rope taut while others take turns jumping over it. Start at ground level, then at shin height, then knees, thighs, hip, waist, under-arm and neck. It's like the limbo, only the exact opposite.

BEST STRATEGY

There are no two ways about it: be tall. The longer your legs, the better.

PHYSICAL RISK — 6/10

Children vaulting over a higher and higher rope can, occasionally, crash and burn.

SURVIVAL TIPS

◆ Play with other kids about your height and agility. Or better still, kids who are much, much smaller than you.

◆ Play on grass; it brings down the injury count if kids aren't landing awkwardly on tarmac, kerbs, etc.

OVERALL PLAYABILITY

This can be a good 'filler' game to play in the downtime between more physical games, like Bulldog or Catch-a-Man.

CONKERS

WHAT YOU'LL NEED

At least two players, and some decent horse chestnuts with a hole through their centre (made by a nail or skewer or other sharp implement) and string or a shoelace threaded through, with a knot tied at one end.

THE BIG IDEA

One player wraps the string around their hand, with the conker dangling at the end, while another tries to hit the conker with their own (using an over-arm swing, aiming their conker down vertically, or opting for a variety of the side slash). First to break the other's conker wins.

Players keep track of how many others a conker has beaten – a none-er, a one-er, a two-er, etc. When a conker destroys another, it inherits all of its wins too, eg when a one-er beats a four-er, it becomes a five-er.

Shout 'Strings!' when the strings tangle and get an extra shot. And shout 'Stamps!' before stamping on any conkers on the ground (or 'No Stamps!' to save your fallen conker).

BEST STRATEGY

- ◆ If you're hoping for a run of victories, make sure your conkers are as symmetrical as possible, and both tough and un-cracked (tip: horse chestnuts that are damaged inside usually float in water, while hardier ones with more potential for Conkers sink). Take care not to damage them when making the hole through them.
- ◆ There are a few (not strictly legit) ways to harden up conkers: drying them out for as long as possible (up to a year – called a seasoner), baking them in the oven or putting them in the 'hot press' or on a radiator, soaking them in vinegar, or even coating them in nail varnish.

PHYSICAL RISK – 4/10

Pushing a nail through a horse chestnut carries some risk and, depending on the age of the children, will require some adult help or supervision. Conkers has been known to register a lot of mis-hits too, depending on the ferocity and skill levels of the players.

SURVIVAL TIPS

Make sure you leave enough string (at least 25cm) when dangling your conker, and hold it out away from your body. Try and ensure that all parts of your body, particularly the softer, squishier bits, are out of the conker-swinging danger zone.

OVERALL PLAYABILITY

Lots of autumn fun, and can be ferociously competitive. The force needed to actually crack a decent horse chestnut means that this is really a game for older kids. Players cultivate their best conkers, and have even been known to pass them on to younger siblings.

CAT'S CRADLE

WHAT YOU'LL NEED

Two players and about 150cm of string, tied together to make a loop.

THE BIG IDEA

This isn't an easy one to describe, so bear with me:

Slip the looped string over your hands, so that all four fingers on each hand are inside it, the thumbs outside.

Loop the string over the four fingers on each hand once again and pull your hands apart, tightening the string.

With your middle finger on your right hand, pick up the string going across your left palm and pull it across.

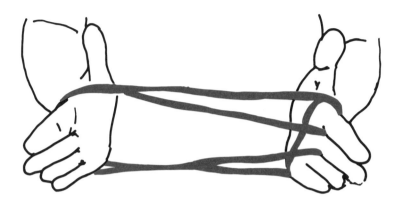

And vice versa (left middle finger, string across the right palm) – making a sort of criss-cross pattern (two crosses and two straight strings).

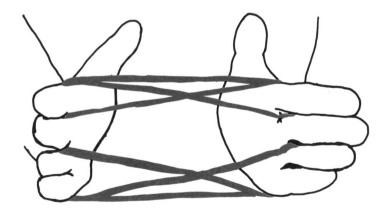

This is called the Cat's Cradle.

RED ROVER, RED ROVER!

Then your friend pinches the two crosses in the middle of the cradle, pulls them up and out, then under the two straight strings, and back up through the space between them.

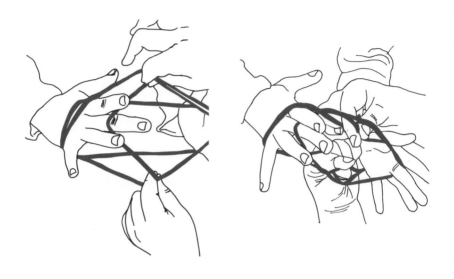

You let go at this stage and they pull the strings tight and – hey presto – the cat's cradle is now on their hands. In theory. In practice, it's probably time to go back and try from the beginning again.

If players do manage to get this far, more advanced string manoeuvres can be used to form other shapes which pass from player to player – the Soldier's Bed, Candles, the Manger, Diamonds, and the Cat's Eye.

VARIATIONS

All alone? Don't fret, you can play this on your own, making shapes such as the Cup and Saucer, Eiffel Tower, Witch's Broom and Jacob's Ladder.

BEST STRATEGY

Let's not beat around the bush – this 'game' is relatively difficult to learn, so is tailor-made for two patient and determined children prepared to spend a considerable amount of time learning it. A lot of trial-and-error is involved, but if you're dead set on learning all the moves, instructional videos are invaluable – get online immediately.

PHYSICAL RISK – 2/10

With hours of practice involved, just watch out for friction burns from the wool or twine.

SURVIVAL TIPS

Make sure you like your Cat's Cradle partner; you need to enjoy nattering away or comfortable silences. You're going to be seeing a lot of each other.

OVERALL PLAYABILITY

The learning is probably the most fun part of this one, or the showing off of it to others. Although once the players know all the set pieces, they can also improvise new formations.

CHASE/ HIDING GAMES

TIG/TAG

WHAT YOU'LL NEED

At least three or four players for the simpler versions, more for Chain Tig, and substantially more for Catch-a-Man/Manhunt.

THE BIG IDEA

One person is 'on' and chases the others. Whoever is caught is then 'on' instead.

VARIATIONS

The fun with Tig is in the variation.

OFF-THE-GROUND TIG

Sort of does exactly what it says on the tin: if you're off the ground (sitting on a wall, hanging from a pillar, clinging to a tree) you can't be caught.

TV TIG

You can't be caught if you jump down on your hunkers and shout the name of a TV programme (which can't be used again in the same game).

STUCK-IN-THE-MUD

When caught the player has to stay exactly where they are, but they stand with legs apart and arms straight out – if another player runs under their arm or between their legs, they're free again.

SHADOW TIG

To catch a player, you jump onto their shadow (and quickly count to three). Only works on sunny days, obviously, and early morning or late afternoon/ evening is best for maximum shadow length.

CHAIN TIG

Each player that's caught holds hands with the one who caught them (again, not romantic in any way). Eventually, there will be a long chain of people running after fewer and fewer people.

CATCH-A-MAN/MANHUNT

Tig for older kids; it's got a much cooler name, and generally involves a lot more roughness when catching. When you're caught, you dust yourself off and join the catcher, roaming the fields/streets in search of the others until everyone's caught. Catch-a-Man can involve a large surface area and take several hours, before everyone gets hungry and goes home for their tea.

BEST STRATEGY

Get away from anyone who's 'on'. Stay away from anyone who's 'on'.

PHYSICAL RISK – 5/10

Risk is largely dependent on the type of Tig you're playing. Catch-a-Man/Manhunt has to live up to its macho name by being a bit rough, while other Tigs are probably hunky dory. Though Chain Tig can involve the person at the end of a chain moving at ferocious velocity as they get dragged around by the others. (It's all to do with rotational physics – look it up.) Believe me, if you've been flung smack bang into a metal pole while at the end of a ten-person chain moving at speed, you won't be quite so keen to play Chain Tig next time.

SURVIVAL TIPS

Limit the chain size for Chain Tig. Or don't play it in a playground with an outdoor shed supported by numerous metal poles.

OVERALL PLAYABILITY

The younger versions of Tig are good holiday fun, but not one to keep kids out of their parents' hair for hours. How long Catch-a-Man lasts is anyone's guess.

BULLDOG

WHAT YOU'LL NEED

A large playing area, or field, and a way of marking the boundaries, either permanent fixtures (trees, lampposts, etc.) or throwing down a few jackets. Best played with a dozen or more children.

THE BIG IDEA

One person is 'on', and stands in the middle of the field. They call the name of another person who must try and run past them from one side of the field to the other. (It's best to have very clearly defined boundaries on all sides.) If the runner is caught, they join the catcher (and are 'on' for the next game), and choose another person to run the gauntlet. If the runner isn't caught – and this is where the full chaotic joy of Bulldog really happens – EVERYONE runs over to them on the other side of the field, with the catcher free to try and catch anyone they can to join them. The game is over when every single kid has been caught.

BEST STRATEGY

This game's not just about being fast, it's about ducking and diving, and finding the best route through possibly hordes of catchers.

PHYSICAL RISK – 7/10

Running from one end of a field to the other shouldn't involve too much risk, but that will depend a lot on who you're playing with. If Tom 'the Rock' Fitzgerald is intent on rugby tackling you to the ground, the chances of a hospital visit are greatly increased.

SURVIVAL TIPS

Keep quiet. If they don't hear you, they won't target you and you can slip past the catchers in the mass migration from one side to the other. This strategy can only keep you safe for so long, though.

OVERALL PLAYABILITY

Highly enjoyable game, and smaller kids can often play well with older ones; they're pretty wily. Length of play has a lot to do with the initial enthusiasm of the kids and whether or not the group includes one homicidal maniac hell-bent on bringing everyone down (you know who you are, Tom Fitzgerald).

COLOURS

WHAT YOU'LL NEED
As for Bulldog.

THE BIG IDEA
This game has a similar set-up to that of Bulldog: one child is 'on', and the others have to run from one well-marked line to another (usually across a field). The person who is 'on' calls out a colour each time – if you're wearing something of that colour (even the teeniest bit of a stripe on your socks, or even underwear), you can swan across in safety. After all the luckily-coloured players are across, the rest have to take their chances and run across without getting caught. When caught, you join those who are on. First caught is on for the next game.

It can be included in the rules that players can bluff in this one – trying to make it across with the first batch of kids wearing the right colour. It's a gamble though, because if there are a lot of people on and you're rumbled, you'll be chased by every single one of them.

BEST STRATEGY
Plan ahead. If you think you're going to be playing Colours that day, wear clothing that is as colourful as possible. Depending on the rules, accessories (hats, scarves, jewellery, hair clips, etc.) are also included. Given an inkling of advance notice, kids playing this game can look like they're lining out for a gay pride parade.

PHYSICAL RISK – 6/10

A lower risk than for Bulldog (because all but the most monochrome children are bound to be able to cross in safety for several turns).

SURVIVAL TIPS

If someone suggests a surprise game of Colours on a day where you're head-to-toe in navy, a bit of sweet-talking might just get you a loan of your best mate's jacket or hair clip. Could save your life.

OVERALL PLAYABILITY

Good fun for a big gang, and fosters wonderful creativity in how kids name the colours they're wearing.

RACES

THREE-LEGGED/EGG AND SPOON/WHEELBARROW

WHAT YOU'LL NEED

Racers in multiples of two for the Three-Legged and Wheelbarrow races. Laces or jackets to tie legs together for the Three-Legged races, and dessert spoons and raw potatoes for the Egg and Spoon.

THE BIG IDEA

There aren't many school activities that kids like to play at home, but we were more than happy to pilfer these races from the school sports day.

THREE-LEGGED

Involves pairs of children, the left leg of one tied to the right leg of the other, trying to make it to the finish line without major injury. (What could possibly go wrong?)

EGG AND SPOON

Each child runs while balancing a potato on a spoon. (Did anyone EVER use an egg for this?) Drop the potato and you have to retrieve it before you can continue.

WHEELBARROW

One kid holds the legs of another who is walking on their hands.

First to the finish line in these races with the pair intact, the potato still balanced on their spoon, or with the wheelbarrow still in operation, wins.

BEST STRATEGY

◆ Evenly matched partners are vital for the Three-Legged and Wheelbarrow races.

◆ Balance and bloody-minded concentration are both required for the Egg and Spoon.

PHYSICAL RISK – 5/10

Competitive races make most kids more reckless than normal, so repeated falls are par for the course. The faster you're going, the harder you fall – smack bang onto your head if you're a poorly-performing wheelbarrow.

SURVIVAL TIPS

◆ Back in our day, we used jackets or t-shirts to tie legs together for the three-legged race. If you do this, make sure the arms of the jacket are wrapped around properly, or there could be some impressive falls.

◆ If you find a parent lenient enough to loan out their dessert spoons and potatoes, make sure you return them in good condition (those spuds are needed for dinner later).

OVERALL PLAYABILITY

Requires a little organisation on the part of an enterprising child or two, but well worth it. A great way to spend an hour.

HIDE AND SEEK/ SARDINES

WHAT YOU'LL NEED

Three or more players, but better fun with half a dozen or so.

THE BIG IDEA

HIDE AND SEEK

The child who is 'on' covers their eyes and counts to a reasonable number (depending on how big an area the game is being played in), then shouts at an unreasonable volume, 'Coming, coming, ready or not, keep your place or you'll be ... *caught!*' They then have to try and find all their hidden playmates, with the last one to be found 'on' for the next game.

SARDINES

Sardines is sort of the opposite to Hide and Seek: just one person hides and everyone else tries to find them. Anyone who finds the hider must hide with them, until one person is looking for everyone else (all crammed into the same place, like the eponymous tinned fish). Last person looking is first hider for the next game.

BEST STRATEGY

◆ There are a couple of sound strategies for Hide and Seek: either find the best hiding place in the world ever, or sneak around from hiding place to hiding place while the seeker isn't looking. Then, remember to stay quiet! Doesn't matter how good your hiding place is if you lead the seeker to you with your muffled giggling.

◆ For Sardines, if you're the hider, take into account that your ingenious hiding place has to accommodate everyone else playing – think big!

PHYSICAL RISK – 3/10

Most of the physical risk in this game comes from kids climbing things they shouldn't – like crumbling garden walls or unsecured wardrobes.

SURVIVAL TIPS

Beware of getting stuck in small spaces, like in cupboard shelves or under beds. (All players know to be on alert for that particular pitch of panicked cry from someone who's just realised they've wedged themselves in somewhere and can't get out.)

OVERALL PLAYABILITY

Can be played inside or out, depending on the weather, children's age, and parents' patience levels. Nicely versatile, and the basis for more advanced hiding games.

FORTY FORTY/ TIP THE CAN/ KICK THE CAN

WHAT YOU'LL NEED

Four or more players (but the fewer the players, the shorter the game), and something to use as 'base' (a pillar, tree or jacket, etc. – originally this was literally a can that players had to kick).

THE BIG IDEA

This game builds on the basics of Hide and Seek. The seeker stands by the base and counts while everyone else hides, then tries to find the others, without straying too far from base. When they spot someone, they run back and touch base, saying that player's name, 'Forty Forty, I see Jenny' or 'Tip/Kick the Can, I see Jenny'.

If Jenny can reach base before the seeker does, she's safe. If not, she's caught and will be on for the next game, unless she is saved by another player. If a player manages to make it to base before the seeker and shout 'Forty Forty, I save all', everyone caught so far is immune from being 'on' for the next game. Worst-case scenario for the seeker is when the last person to be caught swoops in and saves all. If you're the player who manages to do that, it can buoy up your self-confidence for WEEKS.

VARIATION

This game has been updated for new generations with Forty Forty Takedown – a heady combination of Hide and Seek and wrestling.

BEST STRATEGY

You can play a long game by picking a hiding place and sticking to it, in the hope that the seeker will wander far enough from the base to allow you to make a run for it, or you can be a mobile hider, sneaking closer and closer to base before making a surprise attack. Beware other players (like Jenny) blowing your cover by inadvertently (or advertently) alerting the seeker to your position.

PHYSICAL RISK – 5/10

If there's a desperate race to the base between you and the seeker over uneven ground, unexpected obstacles (like rocks, trees or other players) can prove problematic. Add in a possible 'takedown' from the newer version of the game, and the physical risk increases considerably.

SURVIVAL TIPS

◆ Sneakiness is vital for long-term survival in this game.
◆ Younger kids should ideally learn the fundamentals of the game before graduating to Takedown.

OVERALL PLAYABILITY

The more players the better with this one, and older and younger children can play together well. It's not all about strength or speed. If you manage to get a decent crowd together, a good session of Forty Forty/Tip the Can is right up there with the best of them.

Leabharlann na Cabraí
Cabra Library
Tel: 8691

NICK-NACKS/ THUNDER AND LIGHTNING

WHAT YOU'LL NEED

Some gutsy kids (not too many, or you won't all be able to hide nearby) and some unsuspecting neighbours' houses.

THE BIG IDEA

This game has lots of different names, but most Irish children have played it at least once, even the best-behaved amongst us. Once you've been dared to do it, there is no going back. It's simple: ring a neighbour's doorbell and run away. They open the door and there's nobody there. Kids fall about the place laughing.

BEST STRATEGY

Pick your target house carefully. You need to be able to make a quick, unimpeded getaway from the doorstep and have a safe hiding place sussed out nearby.

PHYSICAL RISK — 4/10

The question here isn't really physical harm, but how much trouble you could be in: trespass and disturbing the peace are actually illegal, if the Gardaí wanted to throw the book at you!

SURVIVAL TIPS

Your choice of neighbour has to be the right one. Pick someone who is going to go absolutely nuclear when they realise that kids are pranking them and you're obviously headed for trouble. (I have a vivid memory of one of our neighbours actually legging it up the street after a particularly unfortunate child. Went down in local legend.)

OVERALL PLAYABILITY

This game is not going to last for long, and won't work if repeated often. Half the fun is in the build-up of egging each other on to do it, then laughing about how much fun it was and telling each other how cool you are.

SINGING / CIRCLE GAMES

CLAPPING GAMES (A SAILOR WENT TO SEA)

WHAT YOU'LL NEED

Two players and somewhere quiet to practise.

THE BIG IDEA

The basic action is clap (your hands together), then clap your right hand against their right hand (palm-to-palm), clap, then your left hand against their left hand, clap, then clap both of your hands against the other player's hands three times. Repeat the whole sequence for each line of the song:

A sailor went to sea, sea, sea,
To see what he could see, see, see,
But all that he could see, see, see,
Was the bottom of the deep blue sea, sea, sea.

Subsequent verses replace the words 'sea' and 'see' with another one-syllable word – like knee, toe, chop, etc. – requiring relevant actions instead of clapping (pointing to knee, toe, or chopping action inside the elbow). Children can get as creative as they like with the word they substitute.

VARIATIONS

◆ There are more complicated clapping actions for games like Under a Palm Tree/Under a Bam Brush and Say, Say My Playmate.

◆ These are all two-player games, but you can also play in a circle with players clapping hands with the two players to their left and right – a lot more complicated, and requiring considerable concentration and co-ordination on the part of everyone.

BEST STRATEGY

Practice is essential, but I should warn you that there are people whose clapping skills just won't be up to it.

PHYSICAL RISK – 2/10

This is a sedate game, most often played with two players. But mistakes in the more complicated versions mean that you go left when I go right, resulting in a few bumps here and there.

SURVIVAL TIPS

Similar to Cat's Cradle, it's all about finding a partner with the same hell-bent determination to make this work and free time to practise. If you watch two children who are good at this, they often make the same faces of concentration as those flawlessly jiving couples at weddings.

OVERALL PLAYABILITY

For the best-matched partners, this can not only keep them amused for long periods, it can almost monopolise all of their time.

ORANGES AND LEMONS/ LONDON BRIDGE IS FALLING DOWN

WHAT YOU'LL NEED
Eight or more players (including at least one who knows the song).

THE BIG IDEA
Two players decide between themselves, in secret, who will be 'Orange' and who will be 'Lemon'. Then they stand facing each other, holding hands to form an arch under which the other players skip through as everyone sings the song:

Oranges and Lemons, say the bells of St Clement's
You owe me five farthings, say the bells of St Martin's
When will you pay me, say the bells of Old Bailey
When I grow rich, say the bells of Shoreditch
When will that be, say the bells of Stepney
I do not know, says the Great bell of Bow
Here comes a candle to light you to bed,
Here comes a chopper to chop off your head!
Chip chop chip chop the last man's dead!
(We also used 'Chip! Chop! Cherry!')

On the word 'dead' (or 'cherry'), the two arch players bring their hands down around the player under the arch and, whispering so as the other players can't hear, give them the choice of 'Orange' or 'Lemon' (to keep things interesting, in subsequent rounds, the arch players can pick other choices: 'Chocolate' or 'Strawberry', 'Silver' or 'Gold', etc.). 'Orange' and 'Lemon' teams build up behind the two arch players, holding onto the waist of the person in front of them. When all the players have been picked, the two arch players hold hands and it's tug-of-war time between Oranges and Lemons.

London Bridge is Falling Down follows much the same formula, but with the mercifully shorter song:

London Bridge is falling down, falling down, falling down
London Bridge is falling down, my fair lady

BEST STRATEGY

When you're an arch player, the best strategy is to out-and-out cheat: use a stage whisper when choosing 'Orange' or 'Lemon' so that all your friends (and hopefully the best at tug-of-war) will know to pick you.

PHYSICAL RISK — 4/10

This is largely risk-free playing, although the tug-of-war can involve being collapsed onto by a few of the other kids. And it is possible that 'Oranges' and 'Lemons' could morph into vicious factions.

SURVIVAL TIPS

If you can't survive Oranges and Lemons, maybe playground politics just aren't for you.

OVERALL PLAYABILITY

Singing, skipping, picking one fruit over another – this game has it all. Great fun for younger kids.

RING-A-RING A ROSIE

WHAT YOU'LL NEED

Three or more players.

THE BIG IDEA

A group of children hold hands in a circle and skip around while singing:

Ring-a-ring a rosie,
A pocketful of posies,
A-tishoo, a-tishoo,
We all fall down.

At 'down', everyone falls to the ground.

VARIATION

An extension of the game has another verse:

Mammy in the teapot,
Daddy in the cup,
One, two, three,
And we all jump up!

At 'up', everyone pops back up again, ready for another verse of Ring-a-Ring a Rosie.

DID YOU KNOW?

In the 1980s, it was commonly claimed that this rhyme had its origins in the Black Death – when people carried posies of flowers to ward off the bubonic plague, one of the final symptoms of which was sneezing (before people fell down dead). But this has been debunked more recently, so your little darlings can Ring-a-Ring a Rosie to their hearts' content without fear of conjuring up any morbid images.

BEST STRATEGY

There's an opportunity for parents to take a break during this one. Older children are often happy to lead the younger ones (though they can tend to be a bit rougher when it comes to 'all fall down').

PHYSICAL RISK – 2/10

The risk is in the falling, so just keep half an eye on it.

SURVIVAL TIPS

This is a simple game, only designed to amuse for a few rounds. Be mindful that the longer it goes on, the giddier the children get, and the rougher the circling around and the falling.

OVERALL PLAYABILITY

A fun game for very young children, who will enjoy chanting the rhyme and the simple actions. If you want to keep things going a little longer, you'll need to be ready with a few other games of this type.

THE FARMER WANTS A WIFE

WHAT YOU'LL NEED
A minimum of nine or ten players.

THE BIG IDEA
A group of children form a circle, with one, the 'farmer', in the middle. The circle of children moves around the farmer singing:

The farmer wants a wife
The farmer wants a wife
E-I-addy-oh
The farmer wants a wife

Who do you want for your wife?
Who do you want for your wife?
E-I-addy-oh
Who do you want for your wife?

The farmer picks a 'wife' from the outer circle, and she joins him in the centre (cue lots of whooping and congratulations on the marriage).
The circle moves around them both, singing the same song, but this time 'The wife wants a child'.

After the wife has picked a child (usually with accompanying baby noises), the child wants a nurse, then the nurse wants a dog. The finale is when everyone converges around the dog singing 'The dog wants a pat', patting the nominated dog with varying degrees of accuracy and violence. The dog will be farmer for the next game.

The vaguely sexist tone of this game harks back to a different time, and the feminists amongst us may prefer to adjust the wording accordingly.

BEST STRATEGY
Children usually pick one of their closest friends when it's their turn to choose. If you're going to be centre of attention while a gang of kids circles around you singing, you've got to know someone's got your back.

PHYSICAL RISK – 3/10
The risk here is to the dog, who will hopefully get through the 'patting' without serious injury.

SURVIVAL TIPS
◆ If you're a part of the farming family, grin and bear it. Most children get a bit self-conscious when they're in the middle of the circle, but a couple of rounds of the song doesn't go on too long.
◆ If you're the dog, protect your head.

OVERALL PLAYABILITY
Fun for younger children, probably with a bit of adult supervision. Older children will get more fun out of the whooping at the idea of two of their playmates being married, and slagging another for being the baby – their dog patting is considerably more aggressive too.

DUCK, DUCK, GOOSE

WHAT YOU'LL NEED
A dozen or more players.

THE BIG IDEA
A group of children sit in a circle, and the person who's 'on' walks around the outside of the circle saying 'Duck' for each person as they touch them lightly on the head. When they touch someone and say 'Goose', the goose gets up and runs after them, trying to catch them before they make it all the way around the circle and sit down in the vacated spot. Whoever's left standing is 'on' for the next round.

VARIATIONS

◆ A sweeter version of this game, suitable for even the youngest, is Daisy in the Dell, where everyone stands in a circle holding hands while the person 'on' chants 'Daisy in the dell, I don't pick you ... I do pick you!'

◆ For more daring kids on those summer days, there's Drip, Drip, Drop. One player goes around the outside of the circle with a container of water and 'drips' some on each person's head before 'dropping' the remaining contents on some poor unfortunate. The drenched player tears around the circle to catch the guilty party before they sit down in the space in the circle. Revenge-tastic.

BEST STRATEGY

If you're 'on', use the element of surprise: pick your goose very early in your turn (after one or two ducks), or else leave it for several laps of the circle.

PHYSICAL RISK – 3/10

The two runners are taking the risk in this one, although in the excitement of the final chase it has been known for one or both of them to crash in unexpectedly on top of the other, seated children.

SURVIVAL TIPS

Always be on the alert – for 'goose' or for scrambling runners.

OVERALL PLAYABILITY

Perfect for younger children – it's got suspense and surprise, and the rules couldn't be much easier.

CONCENTRATION

WHAT YOU'LL NEED

Four or more players – the more players, the more entertaining the game is.

THE BIG IDEA

A group of players sit cross-legged in a circle on the ground. Each one is assigned a number, in order as you go around the circle. Then everyone starts a slow clapping rhythm (two slaps on the thigh for each line, followed by two hand claps) to the following chant:

Concentration (slap, slap, clap, clap)
Concentration (slap, slap, clap, clap)
Are you ready? (slap, slap, clap, clap)
If so, (slap, slap, clap, clap)
Let's go! (slap, slap, clap, clap)

Then just the first person takes over, chanting the number 1 for as long as they like and then choosing another number/player, all the while keeping the slapping and clapping rhythm going:
1, 1 (slap, slap, clap, clap)
4, 4 (slap, slap, clap, clap)

At this, player 4 has to pick up immediately, while still staying in rhythm:
4, 4
6, 6

Then it's over to player 6, and so on. The constant throughout the game is the 'slap, slap, clap, clap' rhythm. If anyone misses a beat, or doesn't take over on the beat after their number is mentioned, they're out. Players who are out continue to sit there slapping and clapping, but can't be picked. If you pick one of them when it's your turn, you're out too.

BEST STRATEGY

The title of the game says it all: concentration. You can try and catch other people out by lengthening your turn (repeating '1, 1' for another couple of rounds), but you also need decent rhythm (if you can't keep this going without having all of your concentration on it, you probably won't last too many rounds).

PHYSICAL RISK – 1/10

The game equivalent of yoga. Seriously, there should be no injuries possible here. (And while some adults would struggle to sit cross-legged for too long, kids seem to be able to keep the pose for hours.)

SURVIVAL TIPS

Keep a nice, calm façade. If people can see you're struggling to keep up with the rhythm, you're more likely to get picked.

OVERALL PLAYABILITY

This is a great cool-down or lazy day game for slightly older kids or teenagers. Chances are it won't last too long, unless there are a couple of players determined to out-do one another. In that case, other players tend to get bored and wander off.

TURN-TAKING GAMES

HOPSCOTCH

WHAT YOU'LL NEED

Two players (though you can practise on your own), and a stick of chalk.

THE BIG IDEA

Older than the hills, this one, and there are versions of it played all over the world. Hopscotch can work for a group of children, or be played solo. All you need is a patch of ground where you can draw the recognisable hopscotch grid:

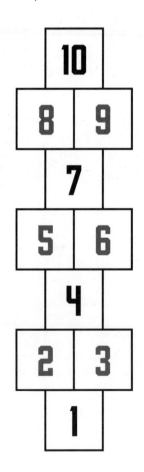

Standing at the bottom of the grid, players take turns throwing a stone into the numbered boxes (starting with 1 and working up), then hopping their way up the grid and back down again. Hop on one leg when there's only one box, and jump with two feet (one on each box) when there are two adjoining numbers. On the way up, you must hop or jump over the box with your stone in it, and on the way back down, stop at the box above it (hop on the 6 box to pick up a stone on 5, etc.) to bend down and retrieve it, before hopping/jumping over it. If your throw doesn't get your stone into the right box, you put your other foot on the ground when you're hopping or picking up your stone, or you jump outside of a box or on any lines, your go is over.

BEST STRATEGY
This game requires a unique blend of stone-throwing and balance. If you can't get your stone into the right box in the first place (which gets more and more difficult with the higher-numbered boxes further away), you'll never be able to show off your insane hopping skills.

PHYSICAL RISK – 2/10
The danger is when over-fatigued hoppers refuse to put their leg down and take a tumble.

SURVIVAL TIPS
No one wants to play this game with an eagle-eyed opponent out to catch you every time your foot strays anywhere near a line. Better to play on a trust basis.

OVERALL PLAYABILITY
This game ranks up there with Sevens for playability. You will end up spending a certain amount of time watching your playmate build up their skill levels. But, in that case, why not draw a couple of Hopscotch grids beside one another?

LETTERS IN YOUR NAME/AUNTIES AND UNCLES

WHAT YOU'LL NEED

At least four players.

THE BIG IDEA

One person is 'on' and stands at one side of the road or other playing area, with their back to all the other players lined up on the other side. They pick a letter: 'Letters in your name ... P (or whatever letter they choose)'. The other players can take a step forward for each P in their name. Then onto the next letter, and the next, until the lucky winner reaches the finish line.

VARIATION

While we didn't play it around our neighbourhood, there's a variation of this called Aunties and Uncles, where you take a step forward for every aunt or uncle you have whose name begins with that letter. This probably worked particularly well for the large extended families of Ireland in the 1980s – although with so many auntie Marys around at the time, there must have been quite a scramble for 'M'.

BEST STRATEGY

◆ The bigger your steps, the less of them you'll need to get to the finish.

◆ After that, it comes down to the number and variety of letters in the name your parents gave you. If your name is something short, like Sam or Tom, best to suggest that everyone uses middle names too.

PHYSICAL RISK — 1/10

Just spelling and walking required for this one.

SURVIVAL TIPS

Favouritism can be a problem with this game. If I'm 'on' and my best friend is Lily Lally, then 'L' is going to be one of the first letters I pick. Outright fixing of the result is minimised by having the person who's 'on' with their back to the others, supposedly unaware of who's winning.

OVERALL PLAYABILITY

Once kids can spell and count, they're well able for this one. Good fun while it lasts, but probably won't last more than a few rounds.

GRANDMOTHER'S FOOTSTEPS/RED LIGHT, GREEN LIGHT

WHAT YOU'LL NEED

A minimum of four players, but better with more.

THE BIG IDEA

All the players stand beside one another at the start line, with the person who's 'on' standing at the finish line. (This can be a definite line, like a kerb, or can be more of a finishing post, like a tree or lamppost.) The aim of the game is to run and sneak up on the person who's on, who has to turn their back to everyone while they say 'Grandmother's footsteps, 1-2-3' or 'Green light, red light'. On '3' or 'Red light', they turn around (at breakneck speed), and everyone has to freeze and stay completely still. If anyone's caught moving, they have to go back to the start line. Then it's time for 'Grandmother's footsteps, 1-2-3' again.

In our version, if you were on, you were allowed to walk down to the other players while they were in statue mode, and try to make them laugh by pulling faces, even tickling them (unless there's a no-touching rule). That paid off a lot of the time, but it meant that players could sneakily move forwards while you were focused on another and also when you were making your way back to your place. You could only send someone back to the start line if you actually saw them move (cue plenty of heated discussion).

BEST STRATEGY

The odds are stacked against fidgety kids in this game. Being able to hold stock-still is by far the most useful skill. But don't underestimate the sneakiness required for advancing on the finish line unseen.

PHYSICAL RISK — 3/10

While there may be some minor risk in trying to hold an awkward pose for too long, the danger in this one is running hell-for-leather for the finish line.

SURVIVAL TIPS

Keep your eye on the long-term objective. Slow and steady really does often win the race here.

OVERALL PLAYABILITY

Great fun, involving a lot of messing, holding back laughter, and sneaking around during the statue phase.

WHAT TIME IS IT, MR WOLF?

WHAT YOU'LL NEED

A minimum of four players.

THE BIG IDEA

The basic set-up is similar to that for Grandmother's Footsteps, but this time the player who's 'on', Mr Wolf, keeps their back to the players until the final stage of the game. Everyone shouts out 'What time is it, Mr Wolf?', and the wolf picks a time, eg 'It's 3 o'clock'. The players take a step forward for each hour (3 steps for 3 o'clock, 5 steps for 5 o'clock, etc.). This is repeated again, and again, until the Wolf decides to cry 'It's DINNER TIME!', and turns around and tries to catch someone before they make it back to the start line. If you're caught, you're Mr Wolf for the next game. But if you reach the finish line before dinner time, you save everyone and the wolf stays 'on'.

BEST STRATEGY

- When you're Mr Wolf, you want to try and gauge how close the players are to you by their voices when they ask the time; they need to be close enough so it's easier to catch them, but not that close to the finish line, obviously.
- For the other players, it's about taking the biggest possible steps, but also being ever-ready to scarper back to the line at a moment's notice.

PHYSICAL RISK — 4/10

There's a wonderful element of panic in this game, when Mr Wolf shouts 'DINNER TIME!', which adds to the risk of injury in the race back home.

SURVIVAL TIPS

Slower runners aren't going to fare the best in this game, in the longer-term. If you're playing with a gang of Usain Bolt wannabes, you should probably resign yourself to being Mr Wolf for quite a few rounds.

OVERALL PLAYABILITY

Plenty to keep kids amused. The nervous anticipation of Mr Wolf calling 'DINNER TIME' is delicious.

MOTHER, MAY I?/ SIMON SAYS

WHAT YOU'LL NEED

At least four players.

THE BIG IDEA

'Mother' stands at the finish line, with their back to everyone for the entire game, while all the other players line up at the start. In our version, whoever was 'on' was always Mother – whether they were male or female – but this game is also played as 'Father, may I?' and 'Captain, may I?'

The object of the game is to be first to make it to the finish, but it's up to Mother how you get there. She picks each player in turn and gives them an action to perform. The player must ask 'Mother, may I?' and get permission first, 'Yes, you may', or they go back to the start (no matter how close to the finish line they are).

The actions are generally one or multiples of the following, all depending on the distance to the finish line and Mother's mood:

Steps	Double steps, baby or giant steps, even backward steps (for the dastardly Mother)
Long jump	Take a great big run up to it
Slow/fast train to Dublin/Cork	You move forward slowly/with speed until Mother says 'stop'

Umbrella	Pretend you're holding an umbrella and move forward while turning around and around (it's one of those things you have to try out, really)
Crawl	Put your hands down as far in front of you as possible, and walk your legs up to them
Crab	Walking sideways, just for the hilarity of it
Squashed tomato	Down on hunkers, waddling forward
Frog/bunny hop	Down on hunkers, then leaping forward (you know, like a frog or bunny)
Lamppost	Lie down flat on the ground, mark where the top of your head is and move to that spot
Banana split	As far as your legs can go towards the splits

Mother's instructions can be as varied or imaginative as you like, as long as everyone is agreed on them beforehand. And with enough variety, it's a great aerobic workout.

VARIATION

This is essentially a much more complicated version of Simon Says, where the person 'on' gives the other players random instructions. The other players must obey only if the command begins with 'Simon says' ('Simon says touch your nose', or 'Simon says stand on one leg'). If you obey a simple instruction ('Touch your nose' or 'Stand on one leg') without hearing those magic words, you're out. Last one out is on for the next game.

BEST STRATEGY

ALWAYS ask permission, like good little children. But after that, the best strategy is to be really, really likeable. This game, similar to real life, is ridiculously open to favouritism. Mother may have her back to everyone, but she knows what instructions she's giving and to whom.

PHYSICAL RISK – 3/10

If you're an awkward mover, watch out for pulled muscles from doing the splits, falls from a failed umbrella, and un-graceful landings after the long jump.

SURVIVAL TIPS

Just try not to overdo the banana split or long jump in your enthusiasm to get to Mother.

OVERALL PLAYABILITY

This one is fun while it lasts, but is so open to fixing that eventually everyone despairs of the blatant unfairness of it. The game was likely developed to teach children to get permission from a responsible grown-up before doing anything, but I'm pretty sure it just makes them resent asking.

SLEEPING LIONS/ DEAD LIONS

WHAT YOU'LL NEED
At least half a dozen players, but will work better with a larger group.

THE BIG IDEA
All but one of the children lie down on the floor and pretend to sleep, or play dead. Once they're still, they cannot move for the rest of the game. The child who's 'on', the 'hunter', prowls around the room trying to make the sleeping lions move by making them laugh (telling jokes, making funny sounds, etc. without actually touching any of the lions). Any lion spotted moving by the hunter must join them on the prowl. The last lion caught is hunter for the next game.

BEST STRATEGY
If you're a lion, find a meditative zen-like state that allows you to block out all external noises and movement. Easy peasy.

PHYSICAL RISK – 2/10
Just be careful you don't split your sides laughing.

SURVIVAL TIPS
It can be difficult for one hunter to survey much larger groups, so they'll need at least one partner in crime.

OVERALL PLAYABILITY
A great game (and a sneaky way) to calm everyone down after more physically demanding activities. A favourite with teachers of younger classes.

SLAPS

WHAT YOU'LL NEED
At least two players, preferably with steady hands.

THE BIG IDEA
One player (let's call them 'the victim') holds their hands out, palms down, over yours, which are palm up. Your object is to slap the back of the victim's hands before they can pull them away. If you do, or if the victim flinches without you trying a hit, it's your turn again. But if you try to slap and miss, it's your turn to be victim. Oh and just to up the ante, if the victim flinches three times in a row before you actually slap, you get to slap them for free. As hard as you like. The game is over when someone can't face the prospect of more slaps, and concedes.

This is a two-player game, but tournaments aren't unheard of. Played all over the place, it's also known as Red Hands, Hot Hands and Flinch – all for fairly obvious reasons.

VARIATION
An alternative set-up has both players with their hands together (as if in prayer, ironically) almost touching at finger tip. In this version, you slap the back of one of their hands using just one of your own.

BEST STRATEGY
While speed and accuracy are important when it comes to scoring a hit, most players are more focused on maximum impact. It's a dog-eat-dog world out there.

PHYSICAL RISK – 9/10

This game is all about physical risk. Be thankful it's only for your hands.

SURVIVAL TIPS

Not one for the faint-hearted. If you have a low pain threshold or don't relish being assaulted in the name of entertainment, this might be a good time to make your excuses and leave.

OVERALL PLAYABILITY

This game is straightforward, controlled violence, so it's easy to see why it's such a big hit with kids (if you'll excuse the pun). For many, it's even better as a spectator sport; tournaments can attract quite an audience.

ENGLAND, IRELAND, SCOTLAND, WALES

WHAT YOU'LL NEED
A minimum of four players.

THE BIG IDEA
Not to be confused with the rhyme used in Elastics, this game needs an area large enough to be divided into four separate sections: England, Ireland, Scotland and Wales. One person is 'on' ('the newsreader') and closes their eyes while the others run to the section of their choice. With eyes still closed, the newsreader makes up today's headline stories (as interesting and implausible as they like), eg 'A meteor hit Scotland, and everyone there lost one eye and one leg, and there was an earthquake in Wales and everyone there lost one arm.' Players in those two countries are now afflicted as described. Then it's time for another round, with the game finishing when someone loses both arms, both legs and both eyes.

BEST STRATEGY
Assuming the person who's 'on' actually does have their eyes closed, this game should be completely random, so you'd better hope luck is on your side.

PHYSICAL RISK — 4/10

Injuries should be imaginary and for the purposes of the game only, but there will always be mishaps when children are hopping around with hands behind their back and eyes closed.

SURVIVAL TIPS

When trying to avoid said mishaps, the skills of hopping and blind navigation do come in useful.

OVERALL PLAYABILITY

Children will enjoy the power of being the newsreader, and there is plenty of fun to be had in gangs of children running, hopping and crawling around with or without the use of their eyes.

POISON

WHAT YOU'LL NEED
At least three players.

THE BIG IDEA
One person is 'on', and holds an index finger of each of the other players. He then tells a very simple story: 'I went to the shop and I bought some ...' and goes on to list the items he bought. When he says 'POISON!' everyone has to run away from him, and whoever he manages to catch is 'on' for the next game. The fun is in the list and how you tell it – best to choose other items that begin with P, so 'I bought ... PENCILS and ... PEANUTS and ... PEACHES and ... POISON!' Great to throw in a bit of 'P ... P ... P ...' before each item, too.

BEST STRATEGY
When you're 'on', do your best to lull everyone into a bored stupor, before pouncing on them with 'POISON!' They'll never be ready to run.

PHYSICAL RISK – 3/10
The panic ups the risk, but there's not too much danger here.

SURVIVAL TIPS
Do some research before the game and find yourself lots of 'P' words. Don't have your vocabulary let you down.

OVERALL PLAYABILITY
Like 'DINNER TIME!' in 'What time is it, Mr Wolf?' kids love the rising excitement of waiting for 'POISON!' As long as they're happy to be on, it is a great game for a grown-up or older child to play with a group of younger children.

COINS

WHAT YOU'LL NEED

At least two players, a wall and some coins (or small stones).

THE BIG IDEA

Players have a handful of small coins each, which they take turns throwing against a wall one coin at a time. At the end of the game, the player who manages to get their coin closest to the wall, wins.

Exact rules can be decided upon before the game starts. Do you have to hit the coin off the wall to have your throw count, or can you just land it close? Another game where deciding whether it's keepsies is important.

BEST STRATEGY

Back in the 1980s when coins didn't spend long in children's hands without being spent (on penny sweets, usually), players could use stones instead. In that case, it's an idea to choose the size and shape of stones to best suit your throw.

PHYSICAL RISK – 2/10

If there's a loose cannon who uses two euro coins and throws like a maniac, there may be some risk. Otherwise, safe as houses.

SURVIVAL TIPS

Try not to spend your entire pocket money on this one. A good way to learn, early on, if you have gambling tendencies.

OVERALL PLAYABILITY

Like any of the other skill-based games, this will depend on how invested you are in it (excuse the pun), and who your playmates are.

POLO

WHAT YOU'LL NEED
At least four players, but gets unwieldy with eight or more.

THE BIG IDEA
Everyone stands at one line, while the person who's 'on' stands at another (short running distance apart). She picks a category – TV programme, colour, comic book character, whatever she likes – and the others all gather together and, whispering, come up with one suggestion each.

All the answers are given to the person on, who doesn't know which answer came from which player. She then calls out one, the owner of which has to race against her (over to the other line and back again, running in opposite directions). The first to get back to their place shouts 'Polo!' and wins.

BEST STRATEGY
◆ If you're 'on', you must try and guess which is the answer from the slowest runner.
◆ If you're one of those coming up with answers, try and pick something funny or quirky, to catch attention.

PHYSICAL RISK – 3/10
The only risk is during the frantic race from line to line.

SURVIVAL TIPS

If there's even a sniff of someone suggesting Polo, immediately say 'I'm bringing them up!' ie bringing the answers up to the one who's 'on'. This is a most coveted role, and will add an extra touch of excitement to your game.

OVERALL PLAYABILITY

Many a happy hour has been spent playing Polo. While a lot of children will stick with the old reliables, the range of categories available is as unlimited as the children's imaginations.

THE HUMAN KNOT

WHAT YOU'LL NEED

The more players the merrier – this is one for large groups.

THE BIG IDEA

There are different versions of this game, but the version we played has one person 'on' who is sent away to count while all of the others join hands in a circle. They must not let go of these hands for the rest of the game. They begin to tangle themselves by sending some players under the chain at different points. Soon enough, it's an unmitigated mess, and that's when the person who's 'on' has to come back and try and untangle the knot by giving directions only: 'Liam, you go under there. Rachel, under there.' etc.

VARIATION

An alternative is to have everyone involved in creating and untangling the knot. Start with all players standing in a circle and joining hands with any two random people, then everyone works together to untangle. The more players the better, this can be a great team-building exercise and ice-breaker.

BEST STRATEGY

There will be some useful strategic thinkers in the bunch who can think a couple of steps ahead. But this isn't really a competitive game and should be a bit of harmless fun.

PHYSICAL RISK — 2/10

The only real risk is wrenching a shoulder when the knot is being untangled.

SURVIVAL TIPS

If you have to choose between your shoulder and the rules of the game, just let go of the hand, man.

OVERALL PLAYABILITY

Good fun for a big gang, both for children and grown-ups, with lots of laughs at the awkward positions everyone gets into. But unlikely to last more than one or two rounds.

CAR GAMES

I SPY/20 QUESTIONS/RED CAR, BLUE CAR

WHAT YOU'LL NEED

A captive audience in the back seat.

THE BIG IDEA

I SPY

A player chooses something within sight of everyone, giving the clue 'I spy with my little eye, something beginning with ... D (or whatever the letter is)'. Whoever guesses correctly goes next. Make sure to choose something that can be seen by everyone in the car for at least a few minutes while the game lasts. For younger players, where spelling may be a problem, try colours instead: '... something that is green'.

20 QUESTIONS

The player who's 'on' thinks of a person, place or thing, and the other players have to ask a series of questions to which the 'on' player can only answer 'yes' or 'no'. First to guess correctly is 'on' next. If no one guesses correctly after twenty questions, the same player stays 'on' for the next round. Variants of this one are Who Am I? (where players choose a famous personality – living, dead or fictional) and Animal, Vegetable, Mineral (where players have to tell the others at the outset which of the three categories what they're thinking of fits into).

RED CAR, BLUE CAR

Each player chooses a colour and gets a point for each car of that colour that passes. Winner is first to a particular score, or the one with the most points at the end of the journey. (A more advanced and modern version of this is to spot car registration plates from the different counties – first to get them all wins.)

BEST STRATEGY

For I Spy and 20 Questions, time to crank that brain up – think obscure! For Red Car, Blue Car, handy to know that silver and black are the most popular car colours.

PHYSICAL RISK – 2/10

As long as everyone's wearing their seatbelts, no safety issues here.

SURVIVAL TIPS

No matter how contentious any of these games gets, no fighting in the back seat. Or you'll walk home.

OVERALL PLAYABILITY

Games that have stood the test of time. A nice bit of distraction for those long drives.

PARTY
GAMES

HALLOWEEN GAMES

SNAP APPLE/APPLE BOBBING/GRAPE IN THE FLOUR

WHAT YOU'LL NEED

An apple threaded onto a string, and a way of hanging it securely. A basin of water and an assortment of apples and coins. A plate or tray, some flour and a supply of grapes.

THE BIG IDEA

SNAP APPLE

An apple hung by string from the ceiling or doorway, and blindfolded children trying to take a bite without using their hands. Sounds easy? It isn't. Apparently modern versions use doughnuts instead of apples, but where is the fun in that?

APPLE BOBBING

A number of apples are put floating in a large basin of water, and children put their arms behind their back and try and catch an apple with their teeth. For added danger (and possible profit) for older kids, our version also had coins along the bottom of the basin, with kids trying to lift them up with their mouth (other versions have the coins actually stuck into the apples). With this one, the water gets everywhere. Do yourself a favour and put down a few towels.

GRAPE IN THE FLOUR

A plate or tray is piled high with flour (you can use a pudding bowl or other mould to make a kind of flour castle, if you like), and a single grape (or sweet) placed on top, in a small dip. Without the use of their hands, children have to bite the grape off without getting flour on their faces. But, as you can imagine, the more flour they get on their faces, the funnier it is.

Another version of this one has children taking turns cutting away part of the flour – whoever causes the pile of flour to fall has to stick their face in and get the grape. For increased mess, do this game after the apple bobbing when the children's faces will still be a bit damp. Or spoil your little ones by using icing sugar instead of flour (because they haven't had enough sugar from the trick-or-treating).

BEST STRATEGY

For Snap Apple, I always found the best technique was to catch the apple between chin and shoulder. Others prefer the full frontal assault.

PHYSICAL RISK – 5/10

Add in an element of coercion and apple bobbing is just water boarding by another name. Only an outside chance of anyone suffocating with their face in all that flour (not to mention the danger to coeliacs). And don't get me started on when that apple swings back and bops you on the front tooth.

SURVIVAL TIPS

When your head's underwater and you're running out of breath, try and keep things in perspective – do you really want a twenty cent coin that much?

OVERALL PLAYABILITY

Money can't buy this kind of fun. These games are what memories are made of.

PASS THE PARCEL

WHAT YOU'LL NEED

The 'parcel' – a small toy or treat wrapped in distinct layers of wrapping paper (the more layers the better) – and as many or as few players as you like.

THE BIG IDEA

Amazing that a lot of this generation of children have never played this one! All the children sit in a circle passing the parcel around while music plays. When the music stops, the child with the parcel takes one layer of wrapping off, then the music starts again. The parcel gets smaller and smaller as you get closer to the toy. The game continues until a child takes the last layer off and wins the prize.

VARIATION

Add a little spice to proceedings by including a small toy or treat in a few of the different layers (before the main prize at the end). Kids will be delighted to win something unexpectedly – this ups the interest level for everyone playing and spreads the joy.

BEST STRATEGY

Maximise the time the parcel is in your hands: take as long as possible to pass it on without everyone complaining, or the person beside you grabbing it out of your hands.

PHYSICAL RISK – 1/10

This should be an injury-free game, though ultimately the game involves one child getting a toy, and everyone else losing. And hell hath no fury like a toddler who keeps getting passed over.

SURVIVAL TIPS

Play nice and be prepared not to win.

OVERALL PLAYABILITY

A great centrepiece for a birthday party – lots of excitement. But smaller children, especially, won't understand why they don't win anything, so there may be tears. Good to have a few grown-ups on hand to referee, or to console.

MUSICAL CHAIRS/ MUSICAL BUMPS/ MUSICAL STATUES

WHAT YOU'LL NEED

Usually best with at least half a dozen players, and a good supply of chairs for Musical Chairs.

THE BIG IDEA

Musical Chairs needs a relatively spacious area to allow for a lot of chairs – one fewer than the number of players – all gathered together in the middle of the room, seat out. The music starts and players walk, dance or prowl around the outside of the chairs. When the music stops (suddenly and unpredictably), everyone must immediately sit on a chair, and the only person left standing is out. For the next round, one of the chairs is removed, and so on until there are only two players and one chair left. When the music stops, the player sitting on the last chair wins.

VARIATIONS

This game can also be played with assigned chairs for each player, and the last to sit down is out. Or forget the chairs altogether and play Musical Bumps, where last to plonk their bum on the ground is out. Musical Statues has everyone dancing to the music, and then freezing when the music stops. The first to move is out, and the music starts up again.

BEST STRATEGY

No matter how upbeat and funky the music is, keep your eye on the prize – stay close to those chairs and ready to pounce.

PHYSICAL RISK – 3/10

The fight for chairs can get a little full-on, so someone can easily end up dumped onto the ground (and a bruised coccyx is nothing to laugh about).

SURVIVAL TIPS

Dancing isn't exactly the key to this game, but maintain a bit of street cred by having some moves ready.

OVERALL PLAYABILITY

A great addition to the party game repertoire, and after a few rounds of this children will probably be ready for something a little less raucous.

MURDER IN THE DARK/WINK MURDER

WHAT YOU'LL NEED

Some paper and a pen, or a pack of playing cards, and enough players to provide the detective with a few likely suspects as well as the actual murderer and the victim.

THE BIG IDEA

Murder in the Dark is best played in a room that is very dark when the lights are turned off. Make up slips of paper for each player, one marked 'Detective', one marked 'Murderer' and all the others marked 'Suspect' (or 'D', 'M' and 'X' to avoid any difficult spelling). Or you can use the required number of playing cards, making sure to include one Ace (for the murderer) and one King (for the detective). Everyone picks a slip of paper or card, and you turn the lights off.

The murderer kills by tapping someone on the shoulder, and the victim falls to the ground, as dramatically as possible. As soon as someone discovers a dead body they shout 'Murder in the Dark!' and the lights are switched on (the murderer should try and 'kill' as many as possible before the lights go back on).

The detective then has to question everyone left alive to work out who the murderer is. (Unless the detective is murdered, in which case – bad luck – the murderer is found out straight away.)

VARIATION

Wink Murder has a similar set-up, except the lights stay on. The murderer kills by winking at someone and the victim leaves the playing area.

BEST STRATEGY

Amateur dramatics make this game all the more fun – time to give in to those dreams of an Oscar.

PHYSICAL RISK – 7/10

A group of kids walking around and dramatically falling down in a darkened room? There's no way that could go wrong.

SURVIVAL TIPS

To limit injuries, we used to send the detective out of the room before all lying down on the floor in the dark. The murderer would crawl around before giving his luckless victim a light tap (but often a good thump), making them scream. When the victim screamed, everyone else jumped up before the detective arrived on the scene of the crime. If you're playing this version, don't give the murderer the satisfaction of a dramatic reaction and they might target someone else next game.

OVERALL PLAYABILITY

A simple whodunit game that can be great fun if everyone gets into the spirit.

BLIND MAN'S BUFF/ SQUEAK, PIGGY, SQUEAK

WHAT YOU'LL NEED
At least four or five players and a blindfold.

THE BIG IDEA
A simple idea: tig with a blindfold. Once the 'blind man' is chosen, they're blindfolded and turned several times, to disorient them. Then the other players can have as much fun as they like calling out to them and ducking away from being caught. In one version, simply catching hold of a player is enough, while in another, the blind man must catch someone and then identify them from feeling their face (and listening to their giggling). Once you're caught, it's your turn to be blindfolded.

VARIATION
A more sedate version of this game is Squeak, Piggy, Squeak. One child, the 'farmer', is blindfolded and given a cushion, while everyone else, the 'piggies', sits in a circle around them. The farmer is spun around three times and then has to make their way to one of the piggies, sitting on them (on the cushion), and instructing the piggie to, 'Squeak, Piggy, Squeak'. The piggie makes a squeaking sound and if the farmer guesses correctly who they are, the piggie is farmer for the next round.

BEST STRATEGY

When you're blindfolded and have someone cornered, stretch those arms out and make yourself as big as you can.

PHYSICAL RISK – 6/10

Blind Man's Buff has 'inevitable injury' written all over it. Less risky when played in a spacious area without dangerous obstacles.

SURVIVAL TIPS

When you're 'on', don't go thrashing around trying to catch people. If you move slowly enough, you'll avoid injuring yourself and also bore the other players into coming closer and closer to you.

OVERALL PLAYABILITY

Children find this game absolutely hilarious. Great for parties.

CHINESE WHISPERS/ RUMOURS

WHAT YOU'LL NEED
The more players, the more pronounced the Chinese Whisper effect.

THE BIG IDEA
Children form a line or circle (the more children, the more fun this game will be), and one thinks up a short sentence. They whisper it to the player next to them, who whispers it to the person next to them, and so on until the final player announces the message to the whole group. The aim of the game is to get the sentence around the group fully intact, but this rarely happens – instead, the final sentence is side-splittingly nothing like the original.

VARIATION
In Rumours, a slightly different version of the game, each player deliberately changes one word in the phrase, preferably to make it funnier (or naughtier).

DID YOU KNOW?
This popular game is named after the process of passing messages along the Great Wall of China.

BEST STRATEGY

◆ There's no winning or losing in this game, it's all about entertainment.

◆ If you're an adult supervising, it's a good idea to have a few sentences ready to go, for any children who are a bit self-conscious about making up their own.

PHYSICAL RISK – 1/10

It's children whispering into each other's ears – does playing get any more gentle than this?

SURVIVAL TIPS

Keep it down – no one likes the Chinese whisperer who can't whisper.

OVERALL PLAYABILITY

A good party game – a few rounds of this will help everyone relax and have a bit of fun.

PEN AND
PAPER
GAMES

FORTUNE-TELLER

WHAT YOU'LL NEED

Paper, a selection of coloured markers or paint and a little imagination.

THE BIG IDEA

Also called a whirlybird, this is a sort of origami game which can seem a bit complicated to construct, but bear with me. First, you need a square piece of paper (a rectangle won't work, so if you've got a standard A4, square it up).

Fold your square paper along one diagonal (corner to corner). Then open and fold along the other diagonal, and open.

 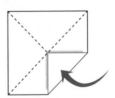

Now fold each of the corners into the centre of the page (where the diagonal folds cross) and, hey presto, you've got another square.

 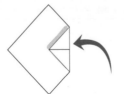

Turn your square over and repeat what you've just done – ie. fold each corner into the centre of the square. That's it – your fortune-teller is made!

Now to colour and write in it. Turn it over and you'll see four small, square petals, each of which you use markers or paints to make a different colour (or just write the name of the colours, if you don't have time).

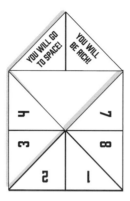

Turn over your square and you'll see four triangular flaps split down the middle, making eight smaller triangles. Number each of these, 1 to 8, then open each flap up and write a 'fortune' to correspond to each number. These fortunes can be in the style of 'You will be rich' and 'You will be married five times', but back in my day we tended to forego fortunes for witty observations and insults like 'You smell like a pig' and 'You have no brain'. Other more sophisticated options are to use dares or riddles.

Get your fortune-teller ready for play by folding the square in half along the centre horizontal, then open and fold in half along the centre vertical. Then put your two index fingers and thumbs under one of the four square petals each. Hold fingers and thumbs together to start, and ask someone to pick one of the four colours on show. Move your fingers and thumbs apart to open the fortune-teller up and back in to the centre again, then open across and back in to the centre, as you spell out the colour, eg B-L-U-E. (This sounds hideously complicated but once you have your fortune-teller in front of you, it'll make more sense.) When you've finished, ask the person to pick one of the numbered flaps they can see inside the fortune-teller. Lift the flap and read what's underneath. Repeat ad nauseum.

BEST STRATEGY

Make sure there's a mix of positive and negative in the comments. No one wants to play with someone who's always dishing out insults.

PHYSICAL RISK – 1/10

The risk here isn't physical, but some of those comments can really hurt your feelings.

SURVIVAL TIPS

Don't get too attached to your fortune-teller. It's only made of paper, so is very susceptible to water, wind, heavy-footed little brothers, etc. One spilled drink and you have to start all over again.

OVERALL PLAYABILITY

Half the fun of this is in the making, half in the playing. Children can take their time and be as imaginative as they like in making the best fortune-teller ever.

BOY, GIRL/ CATEGORIES

WHAT YOU'LL NEED

Pens, paper and two or more players.

THE BIG IDEA

Each player has a piece of paper and a pen. They divide their page into a number of columns (agreed on between the group) and then write subject headings at the top of each one – usually boy, girl, country, fruit, colour, etc. Getting everyone to decide on the categories is half the fun. Kids can go wild and choose singer, movie, cartoon character – anything they like. When all the categories are chosen, one of the players says 'A' and then quietly whispers the alphabet to themselves until another player tells them to stop – whatever letter they have made it to is then used for the first round. For example, if the letter is 'G', all the players have to write down a boy's name beginning with G, a girl's name beginning with G, etc. Once the allotted time is up (agreed at the beginning of the game) players compare their answers. For every answer you have that no one else has, you get 10 points; 5 points for any answer that is doubled up anywhere. Everyone tots up their points and moves on to the next round. Fairly predictably, most points wins.

BEST STRATEGY

- ◆ Try and pick the most obscure answer in each category – you're more likely to get 10 points for Gertrude than you are for Grace.
- ◆ Get everyone to agree to categories that you know a lot about. If vegetarianism is your thing, go for 'Fruit' or 'Vegetable', if you're a sci-fi nerd, push for 'Star Wars character'.

PHYSICAL RISK – 1/10

This is a game for older kids – you need to be able to spell, and count in multiples of 5 and 10 – so you would hope that everyone will be well-behaved and take the game seriously enough without resorting to physical violence. Of course, if you consistently perform badly in this game with your friends, mental scarring is possible.

SURVIVAL TIPS

Pick your playmates wisely. If you think one of them is going to go off the deep end when they're not allowed to use Gammy as a girl's name, best not invite them to play.

OVERALL PLAYABILITY

Excellent. Boy, Girl has been known to last for ages – there are twenty-six letters in the alphabet after all.

CONFESSIONS

WHAT YOU'LL NEED

Pens, paper and two or more (preferably more) players.

THE BIG IDEA

Everyone gets a sheet of paper and starts to write their Confession.
Their crime is broken down under the following:

What did you do? Where? Who were you with? When? What did you do
after it? etc.

After each sentence, you fold down the top of your paper to cover your
answer, and pass your sheet to the next person. At the end, everyone reads
out the combined confession on their sheet. Obviously, the more outlandish
and ridiculous your crimes, the better the game will be.

VARIATION

A broader version of this game has players writing any kind of story (not just
a confession), though the lack of structure can result in just plain zany, rather
than funny.

BEST STRATEGY

The best confessions combine the mundane and the absurd (it was just down
the road, but I was with Homer Simpson), and it's always funny to throw in
authority figures like parents, teachers, etc.

PHYSICAL RISK — 1/10

Just unfortunate pen injuries and paper cuts to watch out for.

SURVIVAL TIPS

Destroy all written evidence after this game. Just in case.

OVERALL PLAYABILITY

One for older kids who won't struggle with all that writing. There are lots of laughs to be had. Play it with your more imaginative and irreverent friends for maximum enjoyment.

X'S AND O'S/ NOUGHTS AND CROSSES/ TIC TAC TOE

WHAT YOU'LL NEED

Pens or pencils, paper and two players.

THE BIG IDEA

One player draws a 3x3 grid (two vertical lines over two horizontal lines), and the two players are each assigned either X's or O's. With X going first, they then take turns placing an X or an O in one of the empty squares until one player wins with three X's or O's in a row (horizontally, vertically or diagonally).

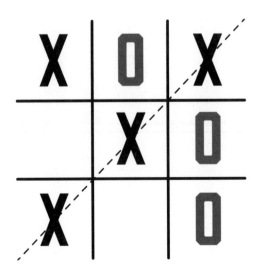

BEST STRATEGY

◆ If the other player starts by placing their X in a corner, always play the centre square. If they start with the centre square, always play a corner square.

◆ Try and create a 'fork' where you can make a row of three in two different ways (eg. take up three of the four corners – your opponent won't be able to block both possible rows).

PHYSICAL RISK – 1/10

Risk-free playing, as long as everyone can handle freshly-sharpened pencils.

SURVIVAL TIPS

◆ Focus on the game in hand. There are thousands of different possible layouts for this game, but with two well-matched players the most likely outcome is a draw.

◆ Feeling the boredom? Up the ante considerably by using a 4x4 grid.

OVERALL PLAYABILITY

Great for younger children to learn the basics of turn-taking, strategic play and low-stakes losing.

DOTS AND BOXES

WHAT YOU'LL NEED

Pens, paper and two players.

THE BIG IDEA

A game for two players (but can be played with more), it starts with a grid of dots. Each player takes turns drawing a horizontal or vertical line between two dots. If one player manages to close a 1x1 box by drawing the fourth line, they put their initial in the box, and take another turn. When all the dots are joined up, the player with more initialled boxes is the winner. Younger children can start off with small grids (say three dots down and three dots across), while the only limit for more advanced players is the size of the paper.

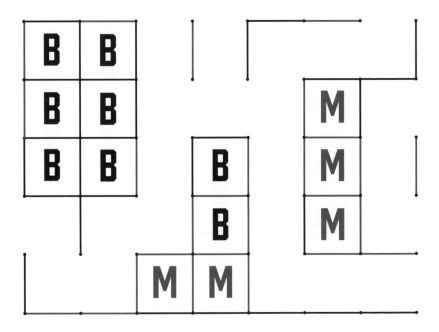

BEST STRATEGY

Thinking strategically is key. You may have to sacrifice one box to get a whole row. Consider your next couple of moves each time, if you can.

PHYSICAL RISK – 1/10

About as dangerous as reading a good book.

SURVIVAL TIPS

Help your self-esteem by picking your opponent well. Nothing as disheartening as playing a seasoned pro and ending up with a sheet of boxes filled with their initial, not yours.

OVERALL PLAYABILITY

A perfect rainy day game – for half an hour at least.

HANGMAN

WHAT YOU'LL NEED

Pen, paper and at least two players (but can work well with a lot more than that).

THE BIG IDEA

One player thinks of a word, and marks a row of horizontal dashes, each one representing a letter in the word. The other players take turns guessing letters that may be in the word. If a guess is correct, that letter is written into the word, wherever it occurs. If a guess is wrong, a line in the traditional Hangman figure is drawn:

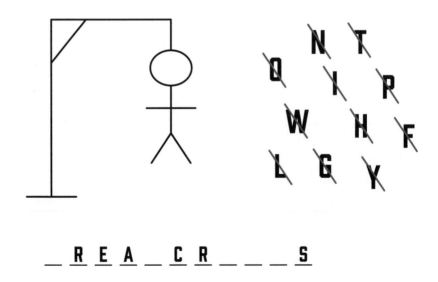

_ R E A _ C R _ _ _ S

Solution: Breadcrumbs

A player may try to guess the whole word at any stage, though an incorrect guess means another element of the Hangman is drawn. Once the Hangman is complete, the game is over.

VARIATION

Versions of the game can use phrases as well as words, use more or less detailed Hangman drawings (some start with the gallows already drawn, others start from scratch) to give the guessers more or less chances to get it right, or outlaw guesses for high-frequency letters like 'e'.

BEST STRATEGY

Pick words without repeated letters, and with a high proportion of consonants and more uncommon letters like z and j.

PHYSICAL RISK – 1/10

Thankfully, the risk is all the hangman's.

SURVIVAL TIPS

Make sure you're playing with people who can actually spell, or you're on a hiding to nothing.

OVERALL PLAYABILITY

This is an absolute classic, and has enough variation to keep everyone happy.

BATTLESHIP

WHAT YOU'LL NEED

Pens, paper (squared pages stolen from a maths copy work really well), and two players.

THE BIG IDEA

Each player has two 10x10 grids on a squared page with numbers 1 to 10 along the top, and letters A to J down the side. One grid is to place your own ships on, the other is to plot your guesses as to where your opponent's are. The ships you have to place are:

1 x Aircraft Carrier (which takes up 5 squares)
1 x Battleship (4 squares)
1 x Cruiser (3 squares)
2 x Submarines (2 squares each)
2 x Destroyers (1 square each)

Once all the ships are placed (horizontally or vertically, not diagonally), it's time to start guessing using the letter and number co-ordinates, e.g. A5, D8, etc. making sure that you note down all the hits and misses on the appropriate grid.

A ship is sunk when all of its squares have been guessed, and the player must announce 'You sank my battleship (or cruiser etc)'. The aim of the game is to sink all your opponent's ships before they do the same to yours.

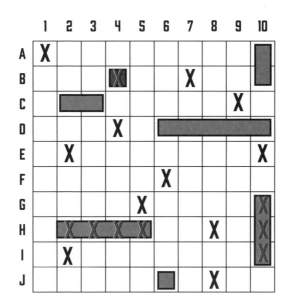

MY BATTLESHIPS

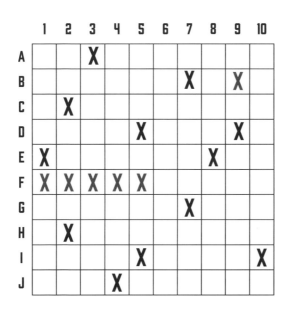

MY OPPONENT'S BATTLESHIPS

VARIATION

There are varying rules for this one, from the number and size of the ships, to not having to declare that your ship is sunk. Players are sometimes allowed an additional guess if they score a hit, or to move their ships between rounds (only for those ships that haven't been hit yet).

BEST STRATEGY

Spread out your fleet. You don't want a player stumbling on your aircraft carrier when they've only just found one of your destroyers.

PHYSICAL RISK – 1/10

Nothing dangerous about jazzed-up coordinate geometry.

SURVIVAL TIPS

Without lucky guesses, Battleship can go on for quite some time. Don't play with someone who's going to get bored and abandon ship after ten minutes.

OVERALL PLAYABILITY

This is one for older children, and you can pepper it with talk of naval manoeuvres and dramatic re-enactment of sinkings but it won't be to everyone's taste.

WHO'S 'ON'?

Of utmost importance at the beginning of a lot of games is picking who's 'on', and there are plenty of ways to do this. When the old reliable 'first come, first served' ('I'm on!/I'm not on!') just won't cut it, there are a few other methods.

Picking straws (or blades of grass) can work. Pick the longest/shortest straw and you're on. More complicated is Rock/Paper/Scissors (rock blunts scissors, scissors cuts paper, paper covers rock), which only works for smaller numbers, and then there is a whole range of rhymes, pointing to a different person for each beat (or to their shoe – remember when everyone had one foot in?).

Happily, most of today's children will be completely unaware of the racist origins of this one (as were most kids back in my day), but if you're uncomfortable with it, why not try the more nonsensical version below:

Eeny, meeny, miney, moe,
Catch a tigger by the toe,
If he squeals, let him go,
Eeny, meeny, miny moe.

Eeny, meeny, ip-a-teeny,
Ah-ba-bu,
Uggly, buggly, boo,
Out stands you.

Or what about this one?

Ibble obble,
Chocolate bobble,
Ibble obble out.

RED ROVER, RED ROVER!

We may have substituted something a bit naughtier for spit in this one. Got a laugh every time.

Ip, dip, dog spit,
You are not it.

In retrospect, this rhyme may well have connotations that were lost on us:

Cinderella, dressed in yella,
Went upstairs to kiss her fella,
By mistake, she kissed a snake,
How many doctors did it take? (Child picks random number, eg 5)
1-2-3-4-5 and out you go.

As well as unnoticed innuendo, quite a few children's rhymes feature what seems to be unnecessary violence:

My mum and your mum were hanging out the clothes,
My mum gave your mum a box on the nose,
What colour was the blood? (Child picks a colour, eg purple)
P-U-R-P-L-E spells purple, and out you go.

One, two, sky blue, it is not you.
Not because you're dirty, not because you're clean,
Just because you're the fairy queen.
O-U-T spells out, and out you go with a jolly good smack across your face.
Just. Like. That. (With or without slow-motion face-smacking actions.)

A bottle of ink fell down the sink,
How many miles did it go?
1-2-3, etc.
O-U-T spells out, and out you go with a doll and a drum,
and a kick in the bum, and a chase around the table.

Another version of this final rhyme had 'Bring your own bread and butter'.
A little less posh, perhaps, but still works:

There's a party on the hill, will you come?
Bring your own cup and saucer and your own cream bun.
Sarah (or other random name) will be there with a ribbon in her hair,
what colour will it be? (Child picks a colour, eg red)
R-E-D spells red and out you go.

MY GAMES

HAD FUN PLAYING THE GAMES IN THIS BOOK, BUT NOTICED A FEW GLARING OMISSIONS?

Use these pages to write down your own favourite games or – even better – paste in photographic evidence.